ROME 2
TRAVEL GUIDE

Your Complete Companion to
Stepping into the Eternal City with
Confidence and Wonder.

By

David M. Taylor

TABLE OF CONTENT

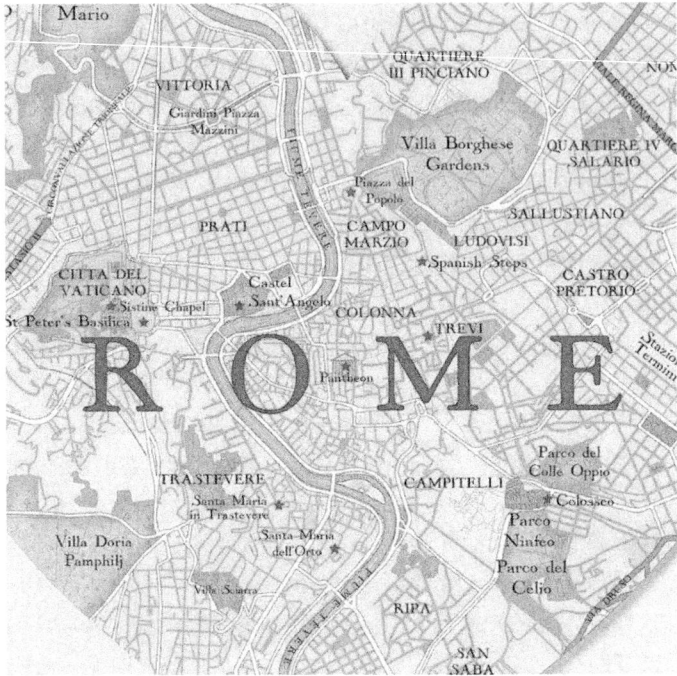

INTRODUCTION

Why Visit Rome?

Rome, called "The Eternal City," is a place where the past and present come together in a unique way. As the capital of Italy, it offers more than just sights—it's a city full of experiences. Everywhere you go, there's a story to uncover, from the days of the Roman Empire to the Renaissance and today's lively culture.

People visit Rome for many reasons. History lovers can explore famous sites like the Colosseum, where gladiators once fought, or the Roman Forum, where emperors ruled. Art fans can admire Michelangelo's paintings in the Sistine Chapel and Bernini's sculptures in the city's fountains. Foodies will enjoy Rome's famous dishes, like pasta carbonara, and the sweet treats of gelato.

But Rome isn't just about its famous landmarks. It's about the atmosphere. The lively piazzas, ancient streets, and small cafes all create unforgettable moments. Toss a coin into the Trevi Fountain, sip an espresso near Piazza Navona, or stroll through the charming neighborhood of Trastevere at sunset. Rome has something magical for everyone.

A Brief History of the Eternal City

Rome has been a major city for over 2,500 years, making it one of the oldest continuously lived-in cities in the world. Its history is like layers of a cake, with stories from ancient times, the Renaissance, and modern Italy all built on top of each other.

- Founding and Legend: According to Roman legend, Rome was founded in 753 BCE by Romulus, a twin who was raised by a she-wolf. This story has become a symbol of Rome's strength and spirit.

- Roman Republic and Empire: Starting in 509 BCE, the Roman Republic introduced laws and systems of government that influenced the world. Later, it became the Roman Empire under Augustus, spreading Roman culture, language, and architecture across Europe, North Africa, and Asia. Famous structures like the Colosseum and aqueducts still stand as reminders of this incredible era.

- The Middle Ages: After the empire fell in 476 CE, Rome became the center of Christianity. It was home to the Pope and played a key role in shaping the faith and power of the Papal States.

- The Renaissance and Baroque Era: Rome came alive again during the Renaissance in the 15th and 16th centuries. Artists like Michelangelo and Raphael created masterpieces that are still admired today, including the Sistine Chapel ceiling. Later, in the Baroque era, artists like Bernini added dramatic flair to the city with works like the Trevi Fountain and Piazza Navona.

- Modern Rome: Today, Rome is the political and cultural heart of Italy. While it celebrates its ancient past, it also thrives with modern museums, trendy restaurants, and a vibrant arts scene.

Rome Through the Ages: Ancient, Renaissance, and Modern

Rome is like a time machine. You can explore its ancient ruins, admire its Renaissance art, and enjoy its modern lifestyle—all in one trip.

1.   Ancient Rome

• Importance: Ancient Rome was the center of one of history's most powerful empires. It introduced systems of law and government that influenced the world. The city spread its culture, language, and ideas across continents.

• Famous Sites: The Colosseum, Roman Forum, Pantheon, and Palatine Hill are must-see landmarks that show the city's impressive history and architecture.

2. Renaissance and Baroque Splendor

• The Renaissance: Rome became a cultural hub, attracting great artists like Michelangelo and Raphael. St. Peter's Basilica and the Vatican Museums are highlights of this era.

• The Baroque Period: This period added drama and beauty to Rome's streets, with landmarks like the Trevi Fountain and Piazza Navona showcasing bold and dynamic designs.

• Cultural Legacy: Art and religion came together in this period, shaping much of Rome's identity.

3.   **Modern Rome**

• A Bustling City: Modern Rome is alive with energy. Ancient ruins stand beside cafes, fashion stores, and lively neighborhoods like Monti and Testaccio.

• Innovation and Style: The city is full of new art galleries, stylish shops, and creative food spots, showing how Rome continues to evolve while honoring its history.

Rome truly offers a blend of the old and the new, making it a city unlike any other.

PLANNING YOUR TRIP

Rome is a city that rewards planning. With its rich history, world-class art, and vibrant culture, making the most of your visit starts with understanding when to go, how to get there, and how to prepare. This chapter provides in-depth guidance to ensure your trip to the Eternal City is seamless and enjoyable.

Best Time to Visit Rome

Rome is beautiful year-round, but the experience varies dramatically depending on the season. Consider these factors when choosing the ideal time to visit:

- **Spring (March to May)**

Spring is one of the most popular times to visit Rome due to the mild weather and blooming gardens. Daytime temperatures range from 50°F to 70°F (10°C to 21°C), making it perfect for outdoor activities and walking tours.

- Events: Spring hosts significant religious celebrations like Easter, with the Pope's Easter Sunday Mass at St. Peter's Basilica drawing crowds.

- Advantages: The weather is pleasant, and the city's many parks, like Villa Borghese, come alive with flowers.

- Drawbacks: Crowds can be heavy around Easter and major attractions. Book accommodations and tickets early.

- **Summer (June to August)**

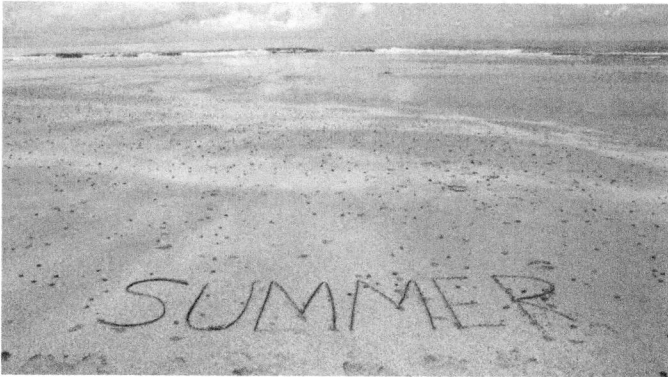

Summers in Rome are hot, with temperatures often exceeding 85°F (29°C) and occasional heatwaves. The city is also at its busiest with tourists.

- Events: Summer festivals include Lungo il Tevere, featuring food, music, and art along the Tiber River. Open-air concerts and outdoor cinema screenings are common.

- Advantages: Extended daylight hours let you explore into the evening, and many landmarks look stunning at night.

- Drawbacks: High temperatures and long queues at major attractions.

- **Autumn (September to November)**

Fall is another fantastic time to visit, with temperatures ranging from 55°F to 75°F (13°C to 24°C). The crowds thin after summer, making it more relaxed.

- Events: The Sagra dell'Uva (grape harvest festival) in nearby Frascati and various wine festivals celebrate the season.

- Advantages: Comfortable weather, fewer crowds, and seasonal food specialties like truffles and chestnuts.

- Drawbacks: Occasional rainy days, so pack an umbrella.

- **Winter (December to February)**

Winter is the quietest season in Rome, except during Christmas and New Year celebrations. Temperatures range from 40°F to 55°F (4°C to 13°C).

- Events: The city sparkles with Christmas lights and markets, and Vatican City hosts special holiday Masses.

- Advantages: Lower prices for hotels and fewer tourists at popular sites.

- Drawbacks: Some outdoor cafes may close, and the weather can be chilly and damp.

How to Get There

Rome is well-connected by air, rail, and road, making it easy to reach from anywhere in the world.

• By Air

Rome's two major airports serve millions of visitors each year:

1. Leonardo da Vinci–Fiumicino Airport (FCO):
• Located 20 miles (32 km) from the city center, Fiumicino is Rome's main international airport.

• Transportation to Rome:
• Leonardo Express Train: A 30-minute direct train to Roma Termini (€14).
• Terravision Buses: Affordable and take about 50 minutes.
• Taxis: Fixed fare of €50–€55 to central Rome.
• Services: Duty-free shopping, lounges, and dining options are available.

2. Ciampino Airport (CIA):
• Located 7.5 miles (12 km) from the city center, Ciampino serves low-cost airlines like Ryanair.

• Transportation to Rome:

- Shuttle buses connect Ciampino to Termini Station (€6).
- Taxis are quicker but cost around €35.
- By Train

Rome is a hub for Italy's high-speed train network:
- Roma Termini: The central station connects Rome to Florence (1.5 hours), Naples (1 hour), and Milan (3 hours).

- Train Classes: Choose between Standard, Premium, and Business classes for comfort and budget preferences.

- International Trains: Routes to Paris, Munich, and Vienna make Rome accessible from Europe.
- **By Road**

Rome is accessible via Italy's excellent highway system (autostrade), but driving in the city can be tricky.
- Parking: Limited and expensive in central Rome. Use public parking garages outside the city center.
- ZTL Zones: Restricted areas for cars in central Rome. Fines apply for unauthorized entry.
- Alternative: Park outside the city and take public transport in.

Visa and Entry Requirements

- Who Needs a Visa?
- Visa-Free Countries: Visitors from the US, Canada, Australia, and many European countries can stay in Italy visa-free for up to 90 days within a 180-day period.

- Schengen Visa: Travelers from other countries may require a Schengen visa to enter Italy.

- Passport Requirements:
Your passport must be valid for at least six months beyond your planned departure date.

- ETIAS Authorization:

Beginning in 2025, travelers from visa-free countries will need to apply for ETIAS (European Travel Information and Authorization System) before visiting.

- Travel Insurance:

Though not mandatory, travel insurance covering medical emergencies is highly recommended.

Packing Essentials for Rome

Packing smart can make your trip more comfortable.
- Clothing:
- Spring and Fall: Layers, lightweight jackets, and scarves.

- Summer: Light, breathable fabrics, a wide-brimmed hat, and sunglasses.

- Winter: Warm coats, sweaters, and waterproof footwear.

- Shoes: Comfortable, supportive walking shoes for navigating cobblestone streets.

- Modest Attire: Churches and religious sites require covered shoulders and knees. A shawl or scarf can be useful.

- Accessories:
- A reusable water bottle to use at the city's nasoni (free water fountains).

- A compact umbrella or raincoat, especially in fall and winter.

- Documents and Money:
- Passports and photocopies.
- Credit cards and some euros in small denominations.

- Electronics:
- Universal adapters (Italy uses Type C, F, and L plugs).
- Portable chargers for your phone.

Rome's timeless appeal makes it a dream destination.

TRANSPORTATION

Rome is a city where history and modernity blend seamlessly, making getting around a fascinating part of the experience. With its ancient streets, modern transport, and varied options, exploring the Eternal City can be straightforward if you understand your choices. Whether traveling to iconic sites, exploring neighborhoods, or venturing beyond the city center, here's an extensive guide to help you navigate Rome like a local.

Public Transportation: Metro, Buses, and Trams

Rome's public transportation network, managed by ATAC, covers the city and suburbs. While efficient and cost-effective, the system requires planning due to traffic, peak hours, and limited routes in some areas.

Metro (Subway)

Rome's metro system is small but efficient, with three main lines connecting major sites and neighborhoods.

- Lines and Coverage:
- Line A (Orange): Links the Vatican Museums (Ottaviano), Spanish Steps (Spagna), and Termini Station, Rome's central transit hub.

- Line B (Blue): Runs from the Colosseum (Colosseo) and Circus Maximus (Circo Massimo) to neighborhoods like EUR and northern areas via the B1 branch.

- Line C (Green): Connects suburban areas to the city, with ongoing work to extend it toward central Rome and archaeological sites.

- Frequency and Accessibility:
- Trains run every 3–7 minutes, with longer waits during off-peak hours.

- Stations often have escalators, but accessibility is uneven. Some older stations lack elevators.

- Operating Hours:
- Sunday to Thursday: 5:30 AM – 11:30 PM

- Friday and Saturday: 5:30 AM – 1:30 AM

- Tickets and Fares:
- Single Ride Ticket (BIT): €1.50, valid for 100 minutes.
- Day Pass (ROMA 24H): €7 for unlimited rides in 24 hours.
- Weekly Pass (CIS): €24 for unlimited rides over seven days.
- Tickets can be bought at metro stations, kiosks, newsstands, and tabaccherie (tobacco shops).

- Metro Tips:
- Validate your ticket at the entrance to avoid fines.
- Avoid peak hours (8–10 AM, 5–7 PM) to escape overcrowding.
- Watch out for pickpockets, particularly at Termini, Spagna, and Colosseo stations.

Buses

Rome's extensive bus system fills the gaps left by the metro, especially for areas like Trastevere, Aventine Hill, and Testaccio.

- Popular Tourist Routes:
- Route 64: Links Termini Station to Vatican City. Convenient but often crowded.

- Route 40 Express: A faster option from Termini to St. Peter's Basilica.

- Route 81: Connects landmarks like Piazza Venezia, Campo de' Fiori, and the Colosseum.

- Operating Hours:
- Day buses run from 5:30 AM to 11:30 PM.

- Night buses (marked "N") operate between 11:30 PM and 5:30 AM.

- Tickets:
- Use the same tickets as the metro. Purchase in advance and validate onboard.

- Tips for Buses:
- Traffic congestion is common, so allow extra time.
- Download apps like Moovit or MyCicero for real-time schedules.

Trams

Trams are quieter and more scenic than buses,
though their routes are limited.

- Key Tram Routes:
- Tram 3: Runs through Trastevere, the
Colosseum, and Villa Borghese.
- Tram 8: Connect Trastevere to
Piazza Venezia.

- Advantages:

- Trams are less crowded and generally more punctual than buses.
- Tickets are the same as those used for the metro and buses.

Walking in the City: Tips and Routes

Walking is one of the best ways to explore Rome's historic center, as many key landmarks are within close proximity.

Why Walk in Rome?

- Most major attractions, like the Colosseum, Pantheon, and Piazza Navona, are within a 30-minute walk of each other.

- Walking allows you to discover charming side streets, artisan shops, and quaint cafes.

- The city's pedestrian zones make walking safe and enjoyable in many areas.

Walking Tips:

1.   Wear Comfortable Shoes: The cobblestones are uneven, so sturdy footwear is a must.

2.   Stay Hydrated: Rome's nasoni fountains provide free, clean drinking water.

3.   Plan Your Routes: Use navigation apps like Google Maps, or carry a paper map for backup.

4.   Traffic Safety: Cross streets at marked pedestrian crossings and be assertive, as Roman drivers can be unpredictable.

Recommended Walking Routes:

1.   Ancient Rome Walk (3 hours):
•   Start at the Colosseum.
•   Walk through the Roman Forum and climb Palatine Hill.
•   End at Capitoline Hill for panoramic views.

2.   Baroque Rome Walk (2–3 hours):
•   Begin at Piazza Navona.
•   Visit the Pantheon.

- Stroll to the Trevi Fountain and conclude at the Spanish Steps.

3. Trastevere Stroll (2 hours):
- Wander Trastevere's cobblestone streets.
- Visit Santa Maria in Trastevere Church.
- End at Gianicolo Hill for a spectacular sunset view.

Renting Cars, Bikes, and Electric Scooters

Cars:

- Avoid renting cars for city travel due to restricted traffic zones (ZTL) and limited parking.
- Best for day trips to areas like Tivoli, Castelli Romani, or the beaches.
- Parking in garages costs €20–€40 per day. Unauthorized access to ZTL zones incurs fines.

Bikes:

- Rentals cost €15–€20 per day; electric bikes are available for hilly areas.
- Best routes include:
- Via Appia Antica: A historic Roman road lined with ruins.
- Villa Borghese Gardens: A peaceful traffic-free area.

Electric Scooters:

• Download apps like Lime or Dott to rent scooters.

• Costs include €1 to unlock and €0.20–€0.25 per minute.

• Scooters are permitted only in bike lanes or streets, not on sidewalks.

Navigating the Fiumicino and Ciampino Airports

Fiumicino Airport (Leonardo da Vinci):

• Rome's main airport, located 20 miles (32 km) from the city center.

• Transport Options:
• Leonardo Express Train: €14, 30 minutes to Termini.

• Regional Train: €8, slower but connects to other stops.

• Shuttle Buses: €6, travel time 50–70 minutes.

• Taxis: Flat rate of €50–€55 to central Rome.

Ciampino Airport:

• Smaller airport serving budget airlines.
• Transport Options:
• Shuttle Buses: €6, 40 minutes to Termini.

- Taxis: Flat rate of €35.

This comprehensive guide ensures you'll navigate Rome with ease, maximizing your experience in the city. Let me know if you'd like further elaboration on any section!

ICONIC ATTRACTIONS

Ancient Rome, the capital of one of history's most powerful empires, is filled with awe-inspiring landmarks that reflect the grandeur, ingenuity, and culture of its time. Visiting these iconic sites not only provides a glimpse into the past but also reveals the advanced engineering, artistic mastery, and societal values that made the Roman Empire a cornerstone of Western civilization. Below is a comprehensive exploration of these significant landmarks, with detailed histories, architectural features, and practical information to enhance your visit.

The Colosseum: A Gladiator's Arena

The Colosseum, also called the Flavian Amphitheater, is one of ancient Rome's most iconic landmarks. Known for its massive size, advanced engineering, and rich history, it is a must-see destination for visitors to Rome. This grand structure was a stage for gladiator battles, animal hunts, and public spectacles, reflecting the grandeur and power of the Roman Empire.

-History of the Colosseum

How It Began

- The Colosseum was ordered to be built by Emperor Vespasian in 70 AD as a gift to the

Roman people. It replaced Nero's private palace and lake, symbolizing the return of public land to the citizens.

- Construction took nearly a decade, and it was completed in 80 AD by Emperor Titus, Vespasian's son. Emperor Domitian, Titus' brother, later made additional modifications.

- The opening ceremony included 100 days of games, featuring gladiator fights, wild animal hunts, and mock naval battles. Over 5,000 animals and countless gladiators participated.

- Its name, "Colosseum," is thought to derive from the Colossus of Nero, a giant bronze statue that once stood nearby.

Purpose and Significance

- The Colosseum was designed as an entertainment venue where gladiators, prisoners, and wild animals fought for the enjoyment of the public.

- It was also a tool for emperors to demonstrate their wealth, power, and generosity, uniting people of all social classes in a common spectacle.

- The games and events were propaganda tools, showcasing the might of Rome and reinforcing the emperor's authority.

-Architecture and Design

The Colosseum is a marvel of Roman engineering and design, with features that made it both functional and awe-inspiring.

Structure and Size

- Shape: The Colosseum is oval-shaped to ensure every spectator had a clear view of the arena.

- Dimensions:
- Height: 48 meters (157 feet), roughly the height of a 15-story building.

- Length: 189 meters (620 feet).

- Width: 156 meters (512 feet).

- Arena Floor: 83 by 48 meters (272 by 157 feet).

- Capacity: It could hold 50,000 to 80,000 spectators, making it the largest amphitheater in the Roman world.

Key Architectural Features

1. Arches and Vaults:
- The Colosseum's 80 arches not only supported the structure but also allowed efficient movement of large crowds.

- These arches provided stability by evenly distributing the building's massive weight.

2. Hypogeum (Underground Tunnels):
- Beneath the arena floor was the hypogeum, a complex network of tunnels and chambers.

- This space housed gladiators, animals, and equipment.

- It featured trapdoors and elevators to bring animals or fighters onto the arena floor for dramatic entrances.

3. Seating Arrangement:
- Seating reflected Roman social hierarchy:

- Elite Classes: Senators and nobles sat closest to the arena.
- Middle Classes: Ordinary citizens sat in the middle sections.
- Women and Slaves: Sat at the very top on wooden benches.

4. Velarium (Awning System):
- A retractable awning made of sailcloth provided shade to most of the spectators.
- Operated by sailors, this advanced pulley system was a remarkable innovation for its time.

5. Materials Used:
- Constructed with travertine stone, tuff, marble, and brick-faced concrete.
- Over 100,000 cubic meters of travertine were used, fastened with iron clamps.

-Events Held at the Colosseum

The Colosseum hosted a variety of events designed to entertain and impress the public while showcasing Rome's power.

Gladiatorial Games

- Gladiators were often slaves, prisoners of war, or criminals trained to fight in specialized schools (ludi).
- They used weapons like swords, tridents, and nets and were matched based on their skill and combat style.
- Popular gladiators could become celebrities, earning fame and, sometimes, freedom.

Animal Hunts (Venationes)

- Wild animals, such as lions, elephants, bears, and leopards, were brought from Africa and the Middle East.
- These animals were pitted against hunters, gladiators, or even each other.
- These spectacles often involved elaborate sets and props, such as trees or miniature landscapes.

Mock Naval Battles (Naumachiae)

- Early in its history, the Colosseum's arena could be flooded to stage naval battle reenactments.
- Combatants fought on boats in simulations of Roman military victories.

Public Executions

- Criminals and prisoners were executed during intermissions, often by being left to face wild animals in the arena.

Reenactments of Historical Battles

- Famous battles were recreated with actors and animals, serving as both entertainment and a reminder of Rome's dominance.

-Decline of the Colosseum

Medieval Use

- After the fall of the Western Roman Empire in 476 AD, the Colosseum was abandoned and fell into ruin.
- It was repurposed as a fortress by noble families and later scavenged for materials to build churches and palaces.

Damage from Disasters

- Earthquakes in 847 AD and 1349 AD caused severe damage, leading to the collapse of parts of its outer walls.

Modern Restoration

- Restoration efforts began in the 18th century under Pope Benedict XIV, who declared it a sacred site to honor early Christian martyrs.
- Today, preservation work continues to maintain its structure for future generations.

-Visiting the Colosseum

Tickets and Admission

- Standard Ticket: €16, includes access to the Colosseum, Roman Forum, and Palatine Hill.
- Special Tickets:
- Hypogeum Access: €22–€35 for tours of the underground tunnels and upper tiers.
- Night Tours: Enjoy the Colosseum illuminated under the stars.

Opening Hours

- Open daily from 9:00 AM until sunset (varies by season).
- Closed on January 1 and December 25.

Getting There

• Metro: Line B, Colosseo Station, is directly across from the Colosseum.

• Bus: Routes 75, 81, and 175 stop nearby.

• Walking: Located within walking distance of landmarks like Piazza Venezia and the Roman Forum.

Tips for Visitors

1. Arrive Early: Visit in the morning or late afternoon to avoid crowds.

2. Book Online: Reserve tickets in advance to skip long lines.

3. Wear Comfortable Shoes: The uneven surfaces require sturdy footwear.

4. Hire a Guide: Learn about the Colosseum's history with a guided tour or audio guide.

5. Stay Hydrated: Bring a refillable water bottle; fountains are available nearby.

Cultural Legacy

• UNESCO World Heritage Site: The Colosseum and Rome's historic center have been UNESCO-listed since 1980.

- Global Icon: A symbol of Rome's enduring legacy, it is one of the most recognized landmarks worldwide.
- Modern Uses: Occasionally used for concerts, cultural events, and causes, such as lighting the Colosseum to highlight global issues.

The Colosseum continues to captivate millions of visitors each year with its rich history, grand design, and enduring legacy. Exploring this ancient amphitheater is a journey into Rome's glorious past, offering a deeper appreciation for its remarkable achievements.

Roman Forum and Palatine Hill

The Roman Forum and Palatine Hill are two of the most important historical landmarks in Rome. These sites were at the center of ancient Roman life, where people gathered for politics, religion, and social events. Together, they tell the story of how Rome rose to power, flourished as an empire, and eventually fell. Here's everything you need to know about their history, main features, and how to make the most of your visit.

What Is the Roman Forum

The Roman Forum was the main public space in ancient Rome, used for government meetings, court cases, religious ceremonies, and markets. It covered a large area filled with important buildings and monuments.

How It Began

- The land where the Forum sits was originally a swamp. In the 7th century BC, the Romans built the Cloaca Maxima, an advanced drainage system, to dry the area.

- Over time, the Forum became the center of public life during the Roman Republic (509–27 BC) and continued to thrive during the Roman Empire (27 BC–476 AD).

What Happened Here?

1. Politics:
- The Curia Julia (Senate House) was where Roman senators debated laws and made decisions about the empire.

2. Law:
- Important legal cases were held in large public buildings called basilicas, such as the Basilica Julia and Basilica Aemilia.

3. Religion:
- Temples like the Temple of Saturn and Temple of Vesta were dedicated to gods worshipped by the Romans.

4. Celebrations:
- Military parades, known as triumphal processions, followed the Via Sacra (Sacred Road) through the Forum to celebrate victories.

Decline of the Forum

By the 4th century AD, the Forum lost its importance as the Roman Empire weakened. Many buildings were abandoned, and during the Middle Ages, the site was used as a quarry for stone.

What Is Palatine Hill?

Palatine Hill is one of the seven hills of Rome and overlooks the Forum. It is famous for being the birthplace of Rome and later the home of emperors and wealthy citizens.

The Legend of Romulus and Remus

According to Roman mythology, Romulus and Remus, twin brothers abandoned as babies, were found and raised by a she-wolf in a cave called the Lupercal on Palatine Hill. In 753 BC, Romulus killed Remus and founded the city of Rome on this hill.

Why Was Palatine Hill Important?

• Homes of the Rich: Palatine Hill became the most exclusive neighborhood in Rome. Wealthy families built large houses here, and during the imperial period, emperors like Augustus and Domitian constructed magnificent palaces.

• Strategic Location: The hill offered views of the Roman Forum, Circus Maximus, and the city, making it a symbol of power and luxury.

What Happened to It?

After the fall of the Roman Empire, Palatine Hill was largely abandoned. Some structures were repurposed, while others fell into ruin. Excavations in the 18th century uncovered much of its grandeur.

Key Highlights of the Roman Forum

1. Temple of Saturn:
• Built in 497 BC, this was one of the oldest temples in Rome, dedicated to Saturn, the god of wealth and agriculture.
• Its ruins include tall columns that once supported the temple's front.

2. Curia Julia:
• This was the Senate House, built by Julius Caesar in 44 BC.
• It's one of the best-preserved buildings in the Forum, with a simple yet impressive design.

3. Rostra:
• A raised platform where public speeches were given.
• It was decorated with prows (rostra) taken from enemy ships as trophies.

4. Temple of Vesta:
• A circular temple dedicated to Vesta, the goddess of the hearth.

• It was cared for by the Vestal Virgins, priestesses who kept the sacred flame burning.

5.   Arch of Septimius Severus:
• Built in 203 AD, this arch celebrates the military victories of Emperor Septimius Severus.
• It is covered in detailed carvings of battle scenes.

6.   Basilica Julia:
• Constructed by Julius Caesar, this large building was used for court cases and public meetings.
• Today, you can see its remains, including parts of the marble floor.

Key Highlights of Palatine Hill

1.   House of Augustus:
• The modest home of Emperor Augustus, featuring beautifully painted walls and floors.
• It reflects his desire to appear humble despite his immense power.

2.   Domus Flavia and Domus Augustana:

- Built by Emperor Domitian, these palaces were used for public ceremonies and private residence.
- They include grand courtyards, fountains, and intricate decorations.

3. Stadium of Domitian:
- A large rectangular space thought to be a garden or an area for athletic events.

4. Hut of Romulus:
- A simple structure marking the mythical home of Romulus, Rome's founder.

5. Cryptoporticus:
- A covered walkway connecting the palaces, adorned with decorative stucco.

-Practical Information for Visiting

Tickets

- A combination ticket grants access to the Colosseum, Roman Forum, and Palatine Hill. It costs €16 for adults and €2 for EU citizens under 26.

Opening Hours

- The sites are open daily, from 9:00 AM until one hour before sunset. They are closed on January 1 and December 25.

How Long to Visit

- Plan to spend at least 3–4 hours exploring both the Forum and Palatine Hill.

What to Bring

- Comfortable Shoes: The paths are uneven and can be steep.
- Water Bottle: Refill it at fountains on-site.
- Sunscreen and Hat: Shade is limited, especially during summer.

Guided Tours

- Hiring a guide or using an audio guide can help you understand the history and significance of the ruins.

Interesting Facts

1. Julius Caesar's Cremation Site:

• The Temple of Caesar in the Forum marks where Julius Caesar was cremated. People still leave flowers there today.

2. Layers of History:
• Many structures in the Forum were built over older ones, showing how the site evolved over centuries.

3. Amazing Views:
• From Palatine Hill, you can see the Roman Forum, Circus Maximus, and even the dome of St. Peter's Basilica in the Vatican.

4. Inspiration for Modern Cities:
• The layout of the Forum influenced the design of public spaces in cities around the world.

Tips for a Great Visit

1. Start Early: Arrive when the site opens to avoid crowds and heat.

2. Plan Your Route: Begin at the Arch of Titus, walk along the Via Sacra, and end at Palatine Hill for the best views.

3.   Visit During Spring or Fall: The weather is pleasant, and there are fewer tourists.

The Roman Forum and Palatine Hill are not just ruins; they are living reminders of Rome's incredible history and influence. Walking through these sites, you can almost hear the echoes of ancient Rome.

Pantheon: Temple of the Gods

The Pantheon is one of the most well-preserved monuments from ancient Rome and a remarkable example of Roman architecture and engineering. Its enormous dome, balanced design, and rich history make it one of Rome's most famous landmarks. Originally a temple honoring all Roman gods, the Pantheon has been used for different purposes over time and is now a functioning Christian church.

Below is a simplified guide covering everything you need to know about its history, structure, and significance.

History of the Pantheon

1. First Construction (27 BC):
- The original Pantheon was built in 27 BC by Marcus Agrippa, a friend and supporter of Emperor Augustus.
- The name "Pantheon" means "all gods" in Greek, reflecting its purpose as a temple for all deities.

2. Reconstruction After Fire:
- The first building was destroyed in a fire in 80 AD. Emperor Domitian rebuilt it, but that structure was damaged again.

3. Current Structure by Hadrian:
- Emperor Hadrian rebuilt the Pantheon between 118 and 125 AD. Unlike earlier versions, it wasn't dedicated to a specific emperor but to all Roman gods.
- Hadrian kept the original inscription on the front: M.AGRIPPA.L.F.COS.TERTIVM.FECIT ("Marcus Agrippa, son of Lucius, consul for the third time, built this").

4.   Conversion to a Christian Church:

•   In 609 AD, the Pantheon became a Christian church called the Basilica of St. Mary and the Martyrs (also known as Santa Maria ad Martyres).

•   This change protected it from damage during the Middle Ages, unlike many other Roman buildings.

5.   Modern Use:

•   During the Renaissance, the Pantheon inspired many architects and became a burial site for important figures like Raphael and Italian kings.

•   Today, it serves as a church and a major tourist attraction.

Architectural Highlights

1.   The Dome:

•   The Pantheon's dome is the largest unreinforced concrete dome in the world, measuring 43.3 meters (142 feet) in diameter.

•   At its center is the oculus, a circular opening 9 meters (30 feet) wide that allows natural light to enter. The oculus symbolizes the heavens and connects the building to the sky.

2.   The Rotunda:

•   The main circular space (rotunda) is perfectly proportioned—its diameter equals its height.

•   The dome gets thinner toward the top to reduce weight, showcasing advanced Roman engineering.

3.   The Portico (Front Entrance):

•   The portico features 16 granite columns, each 11.9 meters (39 feet) tall and weighing around 60 tons. These were imported from Egypt, showing the vast reach of the Roman Empire.

•   The triangular pediment above the columns once had bronze decorations, which were removed in the Middle Ages.

4.   Materials Used:

•   The Romans used concrete mixed with pumice (a lightweight volcanic rock) for the dome.

•   The lower walls were built with heavier materials like travertine, while lighter materials were used higher up to reduce the building's weight.

5.   Marble Floors:

•	The floors have a geometric design of squares and circles, reflecting balance and harmony.

Interior Features

1.	Niches and Altars:
•	The interior has seven large niches, originally designed to hold statues of Roman gods.
•	Today, these niches are used for Christian altars and statues.

2.	Tombs of Famous Figures:
•	Raphael: The renowned Renaissance artist is buried here in a simple tomb that honors his legacy.
•	Victor Emmanuel II: The first king of a unified Italy is buried here as a national hero.
•	Umberto I: Another Italian king, buried alongside his wife, Queen Margherita.

3.	The High Altar:
•	Added after the Pantheon's conversion to a church, the altar is still used for religious services.

Symbolism and Influence

1.	Religious Transition:

- The Pantheon started as a temple for Roman gods, reflecting the inclusivity of Roman religion.
- Its conversion into a church symbolizes the shift from paganism to Christianity in Rome.

2. Architectural Impact:
- The Pantheon inspired many buildings around the world, including:
- St. Peter's Basilica in the Vatican.
- The US Capitol Building in Washington, D.C.
- The Pantheon in Paris, France.

3. Scientific Importance:
- The oculus also acted as a solar clock, with sunlight marking specific times and seasons on the walls and floor.

Tips for Visiting

1. Location:
- The Pantheon is in Piazza della Rotonda, a central square in Rome.

2. Opening Hours:

- Open daily, usually from 9:00 AM to 7:00 PM. Hours may change on holidays or during special events.

3. Admission:
- Entry is generally free, but guided tours or skip-the-line tickets may have additional costs.

4. Best Time to Visit:
- Visit early in the morning or late afternoon to avoid crowds.
- Sunny days provide the best view of the light streaming through the oculus.

5. What to Bring:
- A camera to capture the beautiful design.
- Modest clothing, as the Pantheon is an active church.

Interesting Facts About the Pantheon

1. Rain Through the Oculus:
- The oculus is always open, so rainwater enters but drains away through small holes in the floor.

2. Golden Decorations:

- The original bronze and gold decorations on the roof were removed in the 7th century, some of which were melted down to make parts of St. Peter's Basilica.

3.　Longest-Standing Dome:
- The Pantheon's dome has survived for nearly 2,000 years and remains an engineering marvel.

4.　Continuous Worship:
- The Pantheon has been a place of worship for over 2,000 years, first as a pagan temple and now as a Christian church.

Nearby Attractions to Combine with Your Visit

1.　Piazza Navona: A short walk from the Pantheon, this square features Baroque fountains and street artists.

2.　Trevi Fountain: Toss a coin here to ensure your return to Rome.

3.　Campo de' Fiori: A lively market square perfect for a quick snack or shopping.

Baths of Caracalla

The Baths of Caracalla are one of the most remarkable ancient Roman landmarks. Built during the reign of Emperor Caracalla in the 3rd century AD, they were more than just public baths. They served as a center for socializing, exercising, and relaxation. These baths are a stunning example of Roman architecture, engineering, and luxury.

History of the Baths

1. Construction:
- Built between 212–216 AD under Emperor Caracalla.

• The baths could hold around 1,500–2,000 people at a time, making them one of the largest bathhouses in Rome.

• They were designed as a public amenity to win favor with the Roman people and were free to use.

2. Purpose:

• The baths were not just for bathing. They were places where people could meet friends, exercise, read in the libraries, and even conduct business.

3. Decline:

• The baths remained in use until the 6th century, when invaders cut off the water supply by damaging aqueducts.

• Over time, the site was abandoned and used as a quarry for building materials during the Middle Ages.

Main Features of the Baths

The Baths of Caracalla covered 25 hectares (62 acres) and had distinct sections for bathing, exercise, and leisure.

Bathing Areas

1.   Caldarium (Hot Room):
•   This was a circular, domed room heated by furnaces beneath the floor.
•   It was the warmest area, used for sweating and relaxing.

2.   Tepidarium (Warm Room):
•   A transition room with a moderate temperature between the hot caldarium and the cold frigidarium.
•   It used an underfloor heating system called the hypocaust to keep it warm.

3.   Frigidarium (Cold Room):
•   A massive hall with cold water pools for cooling off after the hot baths.
•   This space featured high vaulted ceilings and beautiful marble and mosaic decorations.

4.   Natatio (Swimming Pool):
•   An open-air pool surrounded by columns, used for recreation and exercise.

Recreational Areas

1.   Palaestra (Gymnasiums):

• Two large courtyards for physical activities like wrestling, weightlifting, and ball games.

2.   Libraries:
• The baths had two libraries—one for Latin texts and one for Greek texts—providing spaces for reading and studying.

3.   Gardens and Walkways:
• The surrounding area featured gardens and pathways where visitors could stroll and relax.

Decorative Features

1.   Mosaics:
• Floors were decorated with intricate mosaics showing geometric patterns, mythological figures, and athletes. Some of these mosaics are now in museums.

2.   Statues:
• The baths were adorned with stunning sculptures, including the famous Farnese Bull and Farnese Hercules, now displayed in the Naples Archaeological Museum.

3.   Frescoes and Marble:

• Walls and ceilings were covered with colorful frescoes and luxurious marble panels.

Engineering Marvels

1. Hypocaust Heating System:
• This underfloor system used furnaces to circulate hot air, keeping the rooms warm.

2. Water Supply:
• Water was brought to the baths through the Aqua Marcia aqueduct, one of Rome's most advanced water systems.

3. Drainage System:
• The baths had a sophisticated drainage system to keep the pools and baths clean and functional.

Significance of the Baths

1. Social Hub:
• The baths served as a meeting place for Romans from all walks of life, promoting interaction and relaxation.

2. Symbol of Power:

• The size and grandeur of the baths displayed the wealth and authority of the Roman Empire.

3. Inspiration for Architecture:
• The Baths of Caracalla influenced the design of later bathhouses and public buildings, including modern architectural projects.

Visiting the Baths Today

1. Tickets:
• General admission costs around €8. Reduced prices are available for EU citizens under 26.
• Some tickets include access to other nearby archaeological sites.

2. Opening Hours:
• The baths are open daily from 9:00 AM to 7:00 PM, with seasonal changes. They are closed on January 1, May 1, and December 25.

3. Getting There:
• The baths are located on Viale delle Terme di Caracalla, about a 10-minute walk from Circo Massimo Metro Station (Line B).

4. What to Bring:

- Comfortable walking shoes for uneven paths.
- Sunscreen and a hat for sunny days.

5. Guided Tours:
- Consider booking a guided tour or renting an audio guide to understand the history and structure of the baths in more detail.

Fun Facts About the Baths

1. Capacity:
- The baths could host up to 1,500 people at once, making them one of the largest bath complexes in the Roman world.

2. Modern Uses:
- Today, the site is used for outdoor concerts and opera performances because of its excellent acoustics.

3. Hidden Tunnels:
- Archaeologists discovered underground service tunnels used to manage the heating and water systems.

4. Artistic Treasures:

• Many statues and mosaics from the baths have been preserved in museums and remain iconic examples of Roman art.

Suggested Itinerary for Visiting

1. Start at the Natatio:
• Begin your tour at the swimming pool area and imagine how Romans used it for recreation.

2. Move Through the Bathing Areas:
• Walk through the frigidarium, tepidarium, and caldarium to experience the full bathing routine.

3. Explore the Palaestra:
• Visit the gymnasiums and imagine the activities that took place there.

4. Admire the Mosaics:
• Take time to observe the intricate floor mosaics that depict Roman art and life.

5. Relax in the Gardens:
• End your visit by strolling through the surrounding gardens and reflecting on the luxury of ancient Roman leisure.

RENAISSANCE AND BAROQUE SPLENDOR

The Renaissance (14th–17th centuries) and the Baroque (17th–18th centuries) were transformative periods in Rome's history. The Renaissance brought back classical ideas like balance, perspective, and focus on human achievements, while the Baroque style was dramatic, emotional, and grand. These eras left a lasting mark on Rome, creating some of its most famous landmarks. This section explores four must-see attractions from these periods: St. Peter's Basilica and the Vatican Museums, the Sistine Chapel, Piazza Navona and Trevi Fountain, and the Borghese Gallery and Gardens.

St. Peter's Basilica and Vatican Museums

-St. Peter's Basilica

What Is It?

St. Peter's Basilica is one of the most important churches in the world and a marvel of Renaissance and Baroque architecture. It was built over the tomb of St. Peter, one of Jesus' apostles, and is the center of the Catholic Church.

History and Construction:
- The original basilica was built by Emperor Constantine in the 4th century but fell into disrepair by the 15th century.

- Pope Julius II ordered its reconstruction in 1506, and it took over 120 years to complete.

- Famous architects like Michelangelo, Bernini, Bramante, and Carlo Maderno contributed to its design.

Features to Look For:
1. The Dome:
- Designed by Michelangelo, the dome is 136 meters (447 feet) tall. Visitors can climb to the top for incredible views of Rome.

2. The Façade and Piazza:
- The wide façade by Carlo Maderno is adorned with statues of Jesus and the apostles.
- Bernini designed the grand St. Peter's Square with 284 columns, symbolizing the Church's welcoming embrace.

3. The Interior:

• Inside, you'll find treasures like Michelangelo's Pietà, Bernini's Baldachin (bronze canopy), and the Confessio, marking St. Peter's tomb.

Tips for Visiting:

• Entry to the basilica is free, but access to the dome costs €10 (elevator) or €8 (stairs).

• Visit early or late in the day to avoid crowds.

Vatican Museums

What Are They?

The Vatican Museums are a vast collection of art and historical artifacts amassed by Popes over centuries. They include masterpieces from ancient Rome, the Renaissance, and beyond.

Highlights:

1. Raphael Rooms:

• These rooms are decorated with frescoes by Raphael and his students, including the famous School of Athens, which celebrates philosophy and classical knowledge.

2. Gallery of Maps:

• A long hallway filled with beautifully painted maps of Italy from the 16th century.

3. Ancient Sculptures:

• Look for the Laocoön Group and Apollo Belvedere, two iconic examples of Greek and Roman art.

Tips for Visiting:

• Tickets are €17. Book online to skip long lines.

• Allow at least 3–4 hours to explore, ending with the Sistine Chapel.

Sistine Chapel: Michelangelo's Masterpiece

What Is It?

The Sistine Chapel is one of the Vatican's most famous treasures. It serves as the Pope's private chapel and the site where new Popes are elected.

Michelangelo's Masterpieces:
    1.   The Ceiling:
- Painted between 1508–1512, the ceiling depicts scenes from Genesis, including the famous Creation of Adam, where God and Adam's fingers nearly touch.
- Michelangelo painted over 300 figures, each incredibly lifelike and detailed.

    2.   The Last Judgment:
- This fresco, painted on the altar wall, shows the second coming of Christ, with souls ascending to heaven or being dragged to hell.

Tips for Visiting:
- No photography is allowed, so take your time to appreciate the details.
- The Sistine Chapel is part of the Vatican Museums, so plan your visit accordingly.

Piazza Navona and Trevi Fountain

-Piazza Navona

What Is It?

Piazza Navona is a lively square built on the site of an ancient Roman stadium. It's known for its Baroque fountains, street performers, and cafes.

Key Features:

    1.   Fountain of the Four Rivers:

    •   Designed by Bernini in 1651, this fountain represents the world's four major rivers: the Nile, Ganges, Danube, and Rio de la Plata.

    2.   Church of Sant'Agnese in Agone:

    •   A Baroque church by Francesco Borromini, located next to the fountain.

Tips for Visiting:

    •   Visit in the evening to see the square beautifully lit and buzzing with activity.

-Trevi Fountain

What Is It?

The Trevi Fountain (Fontana di Trevi), completed in 1762, is Rome's largest and most famous fountain. It celebrates the city's advanced water system and artistic creativity.

Features:

- The central figure, Oceanus, represents water and is surrounded by statues symbolizing health and abundance.
- Legend says that tossing a coin over your left shoulder ensures you will return to Rome.

Tips for Visiting:
- Visit early in the morning or late at night to avoid crowds.

Borghese Gallery and Gardens

-Borghese Gallery

What Is It?

The Borghese Gallery (Galleria Borghese) is a museum inside a former villa, showcasing masterpieces from the Renaissance and Baroque periods.

Art Highlights:

1. Bernini Sculptures:
• Apollo and Daphne: A stunning marble sculpture showing Daphne transforming into a tree.

• The Rape of Proserpina: Famous for its lifelike detail, such as the impression of fingers on flesh.

2. Caravaggio Paintings:
• Includes David with the Head of Goliath and Boy with a Basket of Fruit.

3. Raphael and Titian:
• Look for Raphael's The Deposition and Titian's Sacred and Profane Love.

-Borghese Gardens

What Are They?

The gardens surrounding the gallery are one of the largest parks in Rome, offering a peaceful escape with fountains, pathways, and sculptures.

Highlights:

•   The Temple of Aesculapius by the lake is a picturesque spot.

• You can rent bikes or take a leisurely walk to enjoy the serene environment.

Tips for Visiting:
• Tickets to the gallery must be booked in advance.
• Plan extra time to explore the gardens, especially in spring or autumn.

SUGGESTED ITINERARIES

Rome is a city full of stories at every turn. This three-day plan helps you experience its famous landmarks and hidden gems. Combining ancient history, Renaissance art, Baroque beauty, and local charm, this itinerary promises a memorable trip, whether it's your first or fifth time visiting.

Day 1: Explore Ancient Rome

Morning: The Colosseum and Roman Forum

1.   Colosseum:
•   Start your day early to avoid crowds.

• Discover this famous amphitheater where gladiators once fought, and learn about its impressive architecture.

• Plan for 1.5–2 hours to tour the arena and, if available, its underground areas.

2. Roman Forum:

• Walk to the nearby Roman Forum, the hub of ancient Roman life.

• Don't miss landmarks like the Temple of Saturn, Arch of Septimius Severus, and the Curia Julia (Senate House).

• Spend around 1.5 hours exploring its ruins while imagining the bustling marketplace of ancient times.

Afternoon: Capitoline Hill and Piazza Venezia

1.   Capitoline Hill:
- Visit Capitoline Hill, one of Rome's seven hills, home to the Capitoline Museums. These museums house ancient Roman sculptures and Renaissance masterpieces.
- Admire the Roman Forum from Piazza del Campidoglio, designed by Michelangelo.

2.   Piazza Venezia:
- Walk to Piazza Venezia to see the towering Altare della Patria (Altar of the Fatherland).
- Climb the monument's terrace for panoramic city views.

Evening: Dinner Near Piazza Navona

- Enjoy a relaxing dinner at a trattoria near Piazza Navona.
- Afterward, stroll through the square, admire Bernini's Fountain of the Four Rivers, and soak up the lively atmosphere.

Day 2: Discover Vatican City and Renaissance Art

Morning: Vatican Museums and Sistine Chapel

1. Vatican Museums:

- Begin your day at the Vatican Museums to explore their incredible art collections, including Renaissance masterpieces and ancient treasures.
- Highlights include the Raphael Rooms, Gallery of Maps, and ancient sculptures like the Laocoön Group.

2. Sistine Chapel:
- End your visit at the Sistine Chapel and marvel at Michelangelo's breathtaking frescoes.
- Look out for the famous Creation of Adam and the dramatic Last Judgment on the altar wall.
- Set aside 3–4 hours for this entire experience.

Afternoon: St. Peter's Basilica and Castel Sant'Angelo

1.   St. Peter's Basilica:
•   Visit this world-famous basilica, home to Michelangelo's Pietà and Bernini's grand Baldachin.
•   If you're up for it, climb the dome for unmatched views of St. Peter's Square and Rome.

2.   Castel Sant'Angelo:

- Walk along the Passetto di Borgo, a historic passage connecting the Vatican to Castel Sant'Angelo.
- Explore this ancient fortress and enjoy rooftop views of the Tiber River.

Evening: Sunset at Gianicolo Hill

- End your day at Gianicolo Hill, a peaceful spot for stunning sunset views of Rome's domes and rooftops.

Day 3: Baroque Masterpieces and Local Charm

Morning: Trevi Fountain and Spanish Steps

1.   Trevi Fountain:

•   Start your day at the Trevi Fountain before it gets crowded.

•   Toss a coin over your shoulder into the fountain to ensure your return to Rome.

2.   Spanish Steps:

•   Walk to the Spanish Steps and climb to the Trinità dei Monti Church for views of Piazza di Spagna below.

•   Explore the stylish boutiques and cafes in the area.

Afternoon: Borghese Gardens and Gallery

1.   Borghese Gallery:

•   Spend your afternoon at the Borghese Gallery, where you can see works by Bernini, Caravaggio, Raphael, and Titian.

•   Don't miss Bernini's masterpieces like Apollo and Daphne and The Rape of Proserpina.

2.   Borghese Gardens:
•   After the gallery, unwind in the peaceful Borghese Gardens.
•   Rent a bike or take a leisurely walk through its paths, fountains, and sculptures.

Evening: Explore Trastevere

•   Cross the Tiber River to Trastevere, one of Rome's most charming neighborhoods.
•   Wander through its cobblestone streets, visit Santa Maria in Trastevere Church, and enjoy a relaxed dinner at a local eatery.
•   Wrap up your day with gelato from one of Trastevere's artisan shops.

7-Day Family-Friendly Itinerary in Rome

Rome is a city that offers an unforgettable experience for families with kids of all ages. From ancient ruins and world-famous art to interactive museums and picturesque parks, this 7-day itinerary ensures a perfect balance of history, culture, fun, and relaxation. Each day includes activities that cater to both adults and children, making the Eternal City enjoyable for everyone.

Day 1: Arrival and Introduction to Rome

Morning: Arrival and Check-In

• Arrive at your accommodation and settle in. Choose a family-friendly hotel or apartment near the city center for easy access to major attractions.

Afternoon: Stroll Around Piazza Navona and Campo de' Fiori

• Piazza Navona: Introduce your family to Rome by exploring this lively square. Kids will enjoy watching street performers and admiring Bernini's Fountain of the Four Rivers.

• Campo de' Fiori: Visit the bustling market to try fresh fruits and snacks.

Evening: Dinner at a Family-Friendly Restaurant

• Choose a cozy trattoria with kid-friendly options like pizza and pasta near Piazza Navona.

Day 2: Ancient Rome

Morning: Explore the Colosseum and Roman Forum

• Colosseum: Take a guided family tour to learn about gladiators and ancient games. Kids will enjoy the stories of battles and Roman history.

• Roman Forum: Walk through the ruins where ancient Romans gathered. Use a family-friendly app or guidebook to keep children engaged.

Afternoon: Capitoline Hill and Capitoline Museums

• Visit the Capitoline Museums, which house ancient statues like the Capitoline Wolf. The interactive displays are fun for kids.

Evening: Pizza Night Near Piazza Venezia

• Enjoy authentic Roman pizza at a kid-friendly pizzeria.

Day 3: Vatican City

Morning: Vatican Museums and Sistine Chapel

• Book skip-the-line tickets or a family-oriented guided tour to explore the Vatican Museums. Highlight the Gallery of Maps and Michelangelo's frescoes in the Sistine Chapel for older kids.

Afternoon: St. Peter's Basilica

• Climb to the dome for panoramic views of Rome. The climb is an adventure for older kids, but younger ones can enjoy the views from the square.

Evening: Gelato Stop and Relaxation

• Treat the family to gelato at Old Bridge Gelateria near the Vatican.

Day 4: Baroque Rome and Treasures

Morning: Trevi Fountain and Spanish Steps

• Visit the Trevi Fountain early to avoid crowds. Kids will love tossing coins for luck.

• Head to the Spanish Steps and climb to the Trinità dei Monti Church.

Afternoon: Borghese Gardens

•   Spend the afternoon in the Borghese Gardens, a family-friendly park with open spaces for picnics and play. Rent bikes or pedal boats for a fun activity.

•   Visit the Zoo Bioparco di Roma, a favorite spot for young children.

Evening: Casual Dinner in the Gardens

•   Have dinner at a casual café within the gardens or nearby in the Parioli district.

Day 5: Day Trip to Tivoli

Morning: Villa d'Este

•   Take a short trip to Tivoli to explore Villa d'Este, known for its stunning fountains and gardens. Kids will enjoy the water features and open spaces.

Afternoon: Villa Adriana (Hadrian's Villa)

•   Visit the ancient ruins of Villa Adriana, an UNESCO World Heritage site. The sprawling grounds make it a great place for families to roam.

Evening: Return to Rome and Relax

- Have dinner at your hotel or a nearby restaurant.

Day 6: Hidden Gems and Local Culture

Morning: Trastevere Neighborhood

- Explore Trastevere, a charming area with narrow cobblestone streets. Visit Santa Maria in Trastevere Church, and enjoy a relaxed breakfast at a local café.

Afternoon: Janiculum Hill and Puppet Shows

- Walk up to Janiculum Hill for panoramic views of the city.
- Take younger children to a traditional puppet show at Teatro Verde.

Evening: Dinner in Trastevere

- Enjoy dinner at a family-friendly trattoria. Trastevere is known for its welcoming atmosphere and delicious Roman dishes.

Day 7: Family Fun and Farewell

Morning: Testaccio Food Market

• Visit the Testaccio Market, a less touristy spot where you can taste fresh Italian food and introduce kids to local flavors.

Afternoon: Gladiator School or Cooking Class

• Enroll the kids in a Gladiator School experience, where they can dress up and learn ancient combat techniques.
• Alternatively, take a family cooking class to make pizza or pasta together.

Evening: Sunset at Gianicolo Hill

• End your trip with a quiet evening at Gianicolo Hill, watching the sunset over Rome.

Additional Tips for Families

1. Transportation:
• Use public transport, such as buses and the metro, for short distances. For families with

strollers, opt for taxis or ride-hailing apps when needed.

2.   Dining:
•   Many restaurants in Rome are family-friendly and offer simple, kid-approved meals like pizza and pasta.

3.   Breaks:
•   Include time for rest, especially for young children. Parks like Borghese Gardens or Villa Doria Pamphili are great for downtime.

4.   Essentials:
•   Bring sunscreen, hats, and comfortable shoes, as Rome involves a lot of walking.

CULTURAL AND RELIGIOUS HERITAGE

Rome is a city steeped in culture and religion, often called the "Eternal City" because of its long and layered history. As the epicenter of the Roman Catholic Church and a melting pot of diverse traditions, Rome offers a rich tapestry of cultural and religious experiences. This guide explores its major churches, the Jewish Quarter, important festivals, and local customs.

Here's an expanded and even more detailed account of Santa Maria Maggiore and San Giovanni in Laterano, delving deeper into their history, art, architecture, and unique features. This level of detail will provide a richer understanding of these two magnificent churches in Rome.

Santa Maria Maggiore (Basilica di Santa Maria Maggiore)

Historical Significance

Santa Maria Maggiore has been a cornerstone of Marian devotion since its foundation in the 5th century. Built shortly after the Council of Ephesus (431 AD) declared Mary the Mother of God, the basilica reflects the growing prominence of Mary in early Christian theology. Over the centuries, the church has undergone significant changes, blending its original paleochristian elements with medieval, Renaissance, and Baroque styles.

The basilica also played an essential role during significant historical events. For example, Pope Pius V declared victory after the Battle of Lepanto (1571) here, attributing it to the Virgin Mary. This event further solidified the basilica's reputation as a symbol of divine intervention.

Architectural Highlights

• The Original Structure: Though modified over centuries, the basilica retains its original plan of a large central nave flanked by two side aisles. Its grandeur and layout influenced many subsequent church designs.

• Renaissance and Baroque Additions: Carlo Rainaldi and Ferdinando Fuga added to the basilica's structure during the Renaissance and Baroque periods, making it a fusion of different architectural styles.

Artistic Features

1. 5th-Century Mosaics: The mosaics along the triumphal arch and nave are some of the

oldest Christian mosaics in Rome. They depict episodes from the lives of Moses and Joshua, symbolizing the journey of the faithful.

2. Apse Mosaic: Created in the 13th century by Jacopo Torriti, the apse mosaic depicts the Coronation of the Virgin, surrounded by saints and angels, a masterpiece of medieval art.

3. The Ceiling: The gilded coffered ceiling is a marvel of Renaissance craftsmanship, created under Pope Alexander VI. It is said to be adorned with the first gold brought from the Americas by Christopher Columbus.

4. Chapel of the Blessed Sacrament: Designed by Flaminio Ponzio, this chapel features impressive sculptures and reliefs, demonstrating the richness of Counter-Reformation art.

Relics and Legends

• The Crypt of the Nativity houses relics traditionally believed to be from the manger of Jesus Christ.

• The basilica's legend ties to the miraculous snowfall in August, marking its unique spiritual origin.

Papal Connections

Santa Maria Maggiore is one of the four papal basilicas of Rome. Although the Pope's seat is at St. John Lateran, Santa Maria Maggiore serves as a secondary place for papal ceremonies. Pope Francis, for example, visits the basilica before and after his trips to pray before the Salus Populi Romani icon.

San Giovanni in Laterano (Basilica of St. John Lateran)

Historical Significance

As the cathedral of Rome, San Giovanni in Laterano predates even St. Peter's Basilica. Its significance lies in its status as the first Christian basilica, commissioned by Emperor Constantine after his conversion to Christianity. It served as the residence of popes for over a millennium before the papacy moved to the Vatican. The Lateran Palace adjacent to the basilica was the site of several ecumenical councils.

Over its nearly 1,700-year history, the basilica has survived fires, earthquakes, and invasions, each time being rebuilt or restored, making it a living testament to the resilience of the Church.

Architectural Features

1.   Constantinian Foundation: The original structure was modeled after Roman civic basilicas, repurposed to serve as a place of Christian worship.

2.   Medieval Modifications: After being damaged by fire, the basilica was rebuilt in the Romanesque style.

3.   18th-Century Renovation: Alessandro Galilei's redesign gave the basilica its grand Baroque facade, an architectural triumph that combines classical and Christian elements.

Artistic Highlights

1.   Statues of the Apostles: The twelve colossal statues in the nave are masterpieces of late Baroque sculpture, emphasizing the Church's apostolic foundations.

2.   Mosaics of the Apse: These stunning mosaics, crafted during the 13th century, depict Christ surrounded by saints and symbols of divine glory.

3.   Cloister of the Basilica: The 13th-century cloister, designed by the Vassalletto family, is renowned for its twisted columns and detailed carvings, an example of medieval Romanesque art.

Religious Relics and Sites

1.   Scala Sancta (Holy Stairs): Believed to have been brought from Pontius Pilate's palace in Jerusalem, the steps are a major pilgrimage site. Pilgrims often ascend them on their knees in reverence.

2.   Reliquaries of St. Peter and St. Paul: The high altar contains relics of these apostles, making it a sacred site for the Catholic faithful.

Papal Ceremonies and Legacy

As the Pope's cathedral, San Giovanni in Laterano is the site of major liturgical events, including the annual Holy Thursday Mass. Its inscription, "Omnium Ecclesiarum Urbis et Orbis Mater et Caput" ("The Mother and Head of all Churches of the City and the World"), signifies its unparalleled importance.

Cultural and Spiritual Experience

Visiting these two basilicas provides more than just an appreciation for history and art. They are places of active worship, pilgrimage, and deep spirituality. Attending a Mass or simply spending time in quiet contemplation can be a profoundly moving experience.

The Jewish Quarter and the Great Synagogue of Rome

The Jewish Quarter, also known as the Ghetto Ebraico, is one of the most fascinating and historically significant neighborhoods in Rome. Its narrow cobblestone streets, ancient ruins, vibrant restaurants, and synagogues tell the story of the Jewish community's enduring presence in the Eternal City. At the heart of the Jewish Quarter stands the Great Synagogue of Rome, a monumental symbol of Jewish resilience and faith.

-Historical Overview of the Jewish Quarter

Origins

The Jewish presence in Rome dates back to 161 BCE, making it one of the oldest Jewish communities in Europe. Jewish merchants, diplomats, and later, immigrants arrived from Judea during the Roman Republic. By the 1st century CE, the Jewish population of Rome was well-established, with numerous synagogues and a thriving cultural and religious life.

The Roman Ghetto

In 1555, under Pope Paul IV, the Jewish community was forced to live in a walled-off area near the Tiber River, creating the Roman Ghetto. This area, which measured only about three hectares, housed thousands of Jews in overcrowded and unsanitary conditions. They were subject to restrictions on professions, mandatory attendance at Christian sermons, and heavy taxation.

The ghetto walls were torn down in 1870 when Italy was unified and Rome became its capital. This marked the beginning of emancipation for Roman Jews, though they faced lingering prejudice. Despite centuries of hardship, the Jewish community in Rome maintained its unique traditions, blending Roman and Jewish influences into a distinct cultural identity.

World War II and the Holocaust

During the Nazi occupation of Rome in 1943, the Jewish Quarter was targeted in a devastating raid. On October 16, 1943, over 1,000 Roman Jews were deported to Auschwitz, with only 16 survivors. Today, memorial plaques and stumbling stones (stolpersteine) throughout the neighborhood commemorate the victims.

-The Great Synagogue of Rome (Tempio Maggiore)

Historical Background

The Great Synagogue, built between 1901 and 1904, stands as a beacon of hope and a tribute to the resilience of Roman Jews. After the emancipation in 1870, the Jewish community sought to construct a grand synagogue to symbolize their freedom and religious identity. It was built on the site of one of the five synagogues that existed within the ghetto.

Architectural Features

- Unique Dome: The synagogue's massive square dome, visible from across Rome, is unlike any other in the city. It was deliberately designed to distinguish the building from Christian domes, emphasizing the synagogue's unique identity.

- Eclectic Style: The architecture combines Art Nouveau, Assyrian-Babylonian, and Eastern influences, creating a striking and harmonious design.

- Interior: The interior is richly decorated with vibrant geometric patterns, gilded details, and stained-glass windows that cast colorful light throughout the sanctuary. The intricate mosaics and frescoes highlight the artistic and spiritual heritage of the community.

- Torah Ark: The ark, where the Torah scrolls are kept, is an impressive focal point, elaborately adorned with decorative motifs that reflect Jewish traditions.

Cultural and Religious Significance

The Great Synagogue is not just a place of worship; it is a cultural hub for Rome's Jewish community. It hosts religious ceremonies, concerts, and educational events. It also houses the Jewish Museum of Rome, which preserves the rich history of the Jewish people in the city.

-Key Attractions in the Jewish Quarter

Portico of Octavia (Portico di Ottavia)

Located in the heart of the Jewish Quarter, the Portico of Octavia is a remnant of ancient Rome, built in the 2nd century BCE. Once a grand complex housing temples and libraries, it later became a center for fish markets during the ghetto era. Today, it stands as a striking archaeological site amidst the modern city.

Piazza delle Cinque Scole

This piazza marks the former center of the Roman Ghetto, named after the "Five Synagogues" that existed within the ghetto walls. It is a historic and symbolic space where Jewish life thrived despite the restrictions imposed during the ghetto period.

Fountain of the Turtles (Fontana delle Tartarughe)

This charming Renaissance fountain, located in Piazza Mattei, is a beloved landmark of the Jewish Quarter. Designed by Giacomo della Porta and completed by Taddeo Landini, the fountain features elegant bronze turtles, adding a whimsical touch to the neighborhood.

Kosher Restaurants and Bakeries

The Jewish Quarter is renowned for its kosher cuisine and traditional Roman-Jewish dishes. Iconic eateries like Nonna Betta and Ba' Ghetto serve specialties such as:

- Carciofi alla Giudia: Crispy deep-fried artichokes, a centuries-old delicacy.
- Fritti misti: Fried zucchini flowers and other vegetables.
- Pizza Ebraica: A sweet, dense cake filled with candied fruits and nuts.

The Jewish Museum of Rome

Located within the Great Synagogue, the Jewish Museum offers an in-depth look at the history and culture of Rome's Jewish community. Its collection includes:

- Ancient manuscripts and Torah scrolls.
- Ceremonial objects such as silverware and textiles.
- Artifacts from the ghetto era, including remnants of the old synagogues.
- Exhibits on the Holocaust and the impact of World War II on the Jewish population in Rome.

Modern Jewish Life in Rome

Today, the Jewish Quarter is a vibrant and thriving neighborhood, home to a strong and active Jewish community. It combines ancient traditions with modern life, serving as a cultural bridge between Rome's past and present. Festivals like Yom HaShoah (Holocaust Remembrance Day) and Sukkot (Feast of Tabernacles) are celebrated with communal gatherings, while kosher delis, bakeries, and restaurants continue to preserve and innovate Roman-Jewish cuisine.

Practical Information for Visitors

• Location: The Jewish Quarter is located near the Tiber River, between Piazza Venezia and Trastevere. It is a short walk from the Capitoline Hill and the Theater of Marcellus.

• Great Synagogue Address: Lungotevere de' Cenci, 00186 Rome, Italy.

• Visiting Hours:

• The Great Synagogue and Jewish Museum are open Sunday through Friday. Closed on Saturdays and Jewish holidays.

• Guided tours are available and highly recommended for a deeper understanding of the site.

- Dress Code: Modest clothing is required to enter the synagogue.

- Best Time to Visit: Early mornings or late afternoons to avoid crowds and enjoy the serene atmosphere.

Reflection

The Jewish Quarter and the Great Synagogue are more than historical sites; they are living testimonies to a community that has endured centuries of hardship and thrived despite adversity. A visit here offers not only a glimpse into the Jewish history of Rome but also a profound appreciation for the enduring spirit of this ancient faith and culture.

Festivals and Religious Events in Rome

Rome, the heart of Catholicism and a city with deep spiritual roots, hosts a rich array of religious and cultural festivals throughout the year. These events reflect the city's historical, artistic, and spiritual heritage, drawing millions of visitors and pilgrims from around the world. Below is a detailed exploration of some of the most important festivals and religious events in Rome.

1. Easter Week (Settimana Santa)

When: March or April (dates vary based on the liturgical calendar)

Significance

Easter Week, or Holy Week, is the most important religious period in the Christian calendar, commemorating the passion, death, and resurrection of Jesus Christ. Rome, as the center of Catholicism, hosts solemn and elaborate ceremonies led by the Pope.

Key Events

• Palm Sunday: The week begins with a Mass in St. Peter's Square, where the Pope blesses palm fronds and olive branches.

• Holy Thursday: The Pope celebrates the Mass of the Lord's Supper at St. John Lateran or another major basilica, symbolizing the Last Supper.

• Good Friday: The Pope leads the Via Crucis (Way of the Cross) at the Colosseum, a deeply moving event where the Stations of the Cross are reenacted.

• Easter Vigil (Holy Saturday): This solemn service, held in St. Peter's Basilica, begins in darkness and culminates in the celebration of the Resurrection.

• Easter Sunday: The Pope celebrates Mass in St. Peter's Square, followed by the Urbi et Orbi blessing, addressing the faithful worldwide.

Tips for Visitors

• Arrive early for major events as they attract large crowds.
• Many events are free, but seating may require advance reservations.
• Dress modestly, as these are solemn religious occasions.

2. Christmas Celebrations (Natale)

When: December 24–January 6

Significance

Rome's Christmas season is magical, blending religious devotion with festive cheer. The city is adorned with lights, nativity scenes, and Christmas markets, while the churches host sacred music and Masses.

Key Events

•　Christmas Eve Midnight Mass: Held in St. Peter's Basilica and celebrated by the Pope, this is one of the most attended events of the season.

•　Nativity Scenes (Presepi): Rome is famous for its elaborate nativity scenes, particularly at Piazza Navona, St. Peter's Square, and the Basilica of Santa Maria Maggiore.

•　Feast of the Epiphany (January 6): Marking the visit of the Magi to the Christ child, the holiday is celebrated with processions and festivities, especially in Piazza Navona.

Unique Tradition

•　La Befana: On Epiphany, children eagerly await La Befana, the kindly old witch who delivers sweets or coal, akin to Santa Claus in Italian folklore.

3. Feast of Saints Peter and Paul (Festa di San Pietro e Paolo)

When: June 29

Significance

As the patron saints of Rome, St. Peter and St. Paul are honored with a citywide holiday. Their lives and martyrdom are commemorated with religious ceremonies and cultural events.

Key Events

• Papal Mass: Held at St. Peter's Basilica, led by the Pope.

• Fireworks on the Tiber: A spectacular display near Castel Sant'Angelo.

• Religious Processions: Traditional processions take place in the basilicas associated with the saints, including St. Paul Outside the Walls.

4. Assumption of Mary (Ferragosto)

When: August 15

Significance

The Assumption of Mary commemorates the Virgin Mary's ascension into heaven. It is both a religious holiday and a popular summer festival in Italy.

Key Events

• Masses and Processions: Held in all major basilicas, especially Santa Maria Maggiore, which is dedicated to Mary.

• Cultural Celebrations: Romans often celebrate with concerts, outdoor dining, and fireworks.

5. Corpus Christi (Corpus Domini)

When: May or June (60 days after Easter)

Significance

This feast celebrates the presence of Christ in the Eucharist. Rome's observance is particularly grand, reflecting the city's central role in the Catholic Church.

Key Events

- Papal Procession: Starting at St. John Lateran and ending at Santa Maria Maggiore, this candlelit procession is a beautiful display of faith.

- Eucharistic Adoration: Held in churches across the city.

6. All Saints' Day (Ognissanti)

When: November 1

Significance

This day honors all saints, known and unknown, and is a solemn occasion for prayer and remembrance.

Key Events

- Masses: Celebrated in all churches, with special liturgies in major basilicas.

- Cemetery Visits: Many Romans visit cemeteries to honor deceased loved ones, especially at Campo Verano.

7. Feast of Our Lady of the Snows (Festa della Madonna della Neve)

When: August 5

Significance

This unique Roman festival commemorates the miraculous snowfall in August that led to the construction of Santa Maria Maggiore.

Key Event

• Reenactment of the Miracle: White petals are showered from the basilica's ceiling during a special ceremony, symbolizing the snow.

8. Festival of the Patron Saint of Trastevere (Festa de' Noantri)

When: Late July

Significance

This neighborhood festival celebrates the Madonna del Carmine, the patron saint of Trastevere. It is one of the most lively and culturally rich events in Rome.

Key Events

- Procession: A statue of the Virgin Mary is carried through the streets of Trastevere.
- Cultural Events: Live music, food stalls, and street performances fill the neighborhood.

9. Canonizations and Beatifications

When: Various Dates

Significance

Canonizations and beatifications are major events in the Catholic Church, during which individuals are officially recognized as saints or blessed. These ceremonies often take place in St. Peter's Square, attracting thousands of pilgrims.

10. Pilgrimages and Jubilee Years

- Pilgrimages: Rome is a central destination for pilgrimages, especially during Lent, Holy Week, and other sacred times.

- Jubilee Years: Special holy years declared by the Pope, such as the upcoming Jubilee Year 2025, bring millions of pilgrims to Rome to receive special blessings and indulgences.

Practical Tips for Attending Religious Events in Rome

- Plan Ahead: Major events require early arrival, and some may need reservations.
- Modest Dress: Ensure shoulders and knees are covered when attending church events.
- Public Transportation: Many streets are closed during large festivals; use public transport to navigate the city.
- Local Customs: Respect religious traditions and maintain a quiet, reverent demeanor during ceremonies.

Understanding Roman Traditions and Etiquette

To fully appreciate Rome's cultural and religious heritage, it's essential to understand local traditions and customs.

1. Respect for Sacred Spaces

- Dress modestly when visiting churches and religious sites. Shoulders and knees should be covered.

• Speak quietly inside churches and synagogues to maintain reverence.

2. Roman Greetings

• Italians greet with a handshake or, among close friends and family, a kiss on both cheeks.

• A polite "Buongiorno" (Good morning) or "Buonasera" (Good evening) is appreciated when entering shops or restaurants.

3. Dining Etiquette

• Meals are a cherished tradition in Rome. Take your time to enjoy the experience.

• Bread is often served without butter or olive oil. Avoid asking for it unless it's part of the meal.

4. Tipping

• Tipping is not mandatory but appreciated. Leave a small tip for excellent service (5–10%).

5. Festivals and Public Holidays

- During major festivals, public transport and attractions may have limited hours. Plan ahead to avoid disruptions.

FOOD AND DRINK

Rome's food culture is rooted in tradition, simplicity, and bold flavors. Centuries-old recipes continue to define the city's culinary identity, offering dishes that highlight the rich history of Roman cuisine. Whether enjoying a plate of pasta at a trattoria, savoring gelato by a piazza, or sipping wine during aperitivo, every bite is an experience to remember. Here's an in-depth look at Rome's must-try dishes, top dining spots, and food culture.

Iconic Roman Dishes You Must Try

1. Pasta Dishes

Roman pastas are world-famous for their bold flavors, made with simple yet high-quality ingredients:

- Carbonara: A creamy dish made with eggs, pecorino cheese, guanciale (cured pork cheek), and black pepper, traditionally served with spaghetti or rigatoni.

• Cacio e Pepe: Meaning "cheese and pepper," this pasta is made with pecorino cheese and black pepper, creating a rich, silky sauce.

• Amatriciana: A tomato-based pasta enriched with guanciale and pecorino, often paired with bucatini or rigatoni.

• Gricia: Known as the "white Amatriciana," this dish skips the tomato but retains guanciale and pecorino for a savory flavor.

2. Main Courses (Secondi)

Secondi highlight Rome's historic love for hearty, flavorful meats:

- Saltimbocca alla Romana: Tender veal slices topped with prosciutto and sage, cooked in white wine and butter.

• Coda alla Vaccinara: A rich, slow-cooked oxtail stew with celery, carrots, and tomato sauce.

• Abbacchio alla Scottadito: Grilled lamb chops flavored with rosemary, olive oil, and garlic.

3. Street Food and Snacks

Rome's street food offers quick and delicious bites for travelers on the go:

- Supplì: Fried rice balls filled with mozzarella and, sometimes, ragù.

- Trapizzino: A triangular pizza pocket stuffed with Roman classics like meatballs or chicken cacciatore.

- Porchetta: Herb-roasted pork sliced and served in sandwiches, loved for its crispy skin and tender meat.

4. Desserts and Pastries

Sweet treats in Rome are simple yet indulgent:

- Maritozzo: A soft brioche bun filled with fresh whipped cream.

- Tiramisu: Although not Roman, this coffee-flavored dessert is a local favorite.

- Pangiallo Romano: A traditional Christmas cake made with dried fruits, honey, and nuts.

Best Cafés, Trattorias, and Gelaterias

1. Best Cafés

Coffee is a daily ritual in Rome, with iconic spots offering both history and quality:

•   Sant'Eustachio Il Caffè: Famous for its secret coffee blend and creamy espresso.

- Tazza d'Oro: Located near the Pantheon, known for its granita di caffè (iced coffee with cream).

- Caffè Greco: Rome's oldest café, filled with historic charm on Via dei Condotti.

2. Best Trattorias and Restaurants

Trattorias are perfect for savoring Roman classics in a welcoming atmosphere:
- Roscioli Salumeria con Cucina: Renowned for its carbonara and extensive wine collection.

- Armando al Pantheon: A family-run trattoria near the Pantheon serving authentic Roman dishes.

- Flavio al Velavevodetto: Located in Testaccio, it's known for its hearty cacio e pepe.

- Da Enzo al 29: A cozy Trastevere spot famous for its amatriciana and fried artichokes.

3. Best Gelaterias

Gelato is an essential Roman treat, with artisanal shops offering creative flavors:
- Gelateria del Teatro: Unique options like rosemary-honey-lemon.

- Fatamorgana: Known for natural, creative flavors like fig and balsamic.

- Otaleg!: A quirky shop in Monteverde with inventive gelato variations.

- Giolitti: One of Rome's oldest and most famous gelaterias near the Pantheon.

Wine and Aperitivo Culture

Wine in Rome

Italian wines, including those from nearby Lazio, are an essential part of Roman dining:

- Frascati: A crisp white wine often paired with Roman dishes.
- Cesanese: A robust red wine ideal for meat-based meals.

- Chianti and Montepulciano: Popular wines from Tuscany and Abruzzo, frequently enjoyed in Rome.

Aperitivo Tradition

Aperitivo is a cherished pre-dinner tradition in Rome, offering light snacks with drinks:

• Spritz: A refreshing mix of Prosecco, Aperol, and soda water.

• Negroni: A bold cocktail of gin, Campari, and sweet vermouth.

• Snacks: Small plates like olives, bruschetta, and charcuterie.

Top Aperitivo Spots:

• Freni e Frizioni: A vibrant Trastevere spot for creative cocktails.

• Il Goccetto: A cozy wine bar in Campo de' Fiori.

• Bar del Fico: Perfect for people-watching with a classic spritz.

Markets and Food Tours in Rome

1. Best Food Markets

Markets are a great way to connect with local ingredients and culinary traditions:

• Campo de' Fiori: A lively market offering fresh produce, spices, and local treats.

• Mercato di Testaccio: Known for its variety of food stalls, including trapizzino and supplì.

• Nuovo Mercato Esquilino: A multicultural market with ingredients from around the world.

2. Food Tours

Food tours are an excellent way to explore Rome's culinary scene:

• Trastevere Food Tour: Enjoy local specialties like fried artichokes and supplì in this picturesque neighborhood.

• Testaccio Market Tour: Dive into Roman food traditions while sampling fresh ingredients and street food.

• Pasta-Making Classes: Learn to make classic Roman pastas like carbonara and cacio e pepe with expert chefs.

Tips for Enjoying Food in Rome

1.   Eat Seasonally: Roman cuisine is based on fresh, seasonal ingredients. Try artichokes in spring and puntarelle in winter.

2.   Avoid Tourist Traps: Look for restaurants filled with locals and menus in Italian.

3.   Take Your Time: Meals are a slow and enjoyable experience in Rome. Don't rush.

4.   Know the Basics: Stand at the bar to drink coffee for a quick, affordable experience.

HIDDEN GEMS AND OFF-THE-BEATEN PATH

Rome is world-renowned for its landmarks like the Colosseum, Vatican City, and Trevi Fountain, but the city has so much more to offer beyond these iconic sites. For travelers seeking a unique experience, Rome's hidden gems reveal its quieter corners, intriguing history, and modern cultural energy. These lesser-known treasures showcase the city's depth, combining history, art, and daily life.

Aventine Keyhole and Orange Garden

Aventine Keyhole

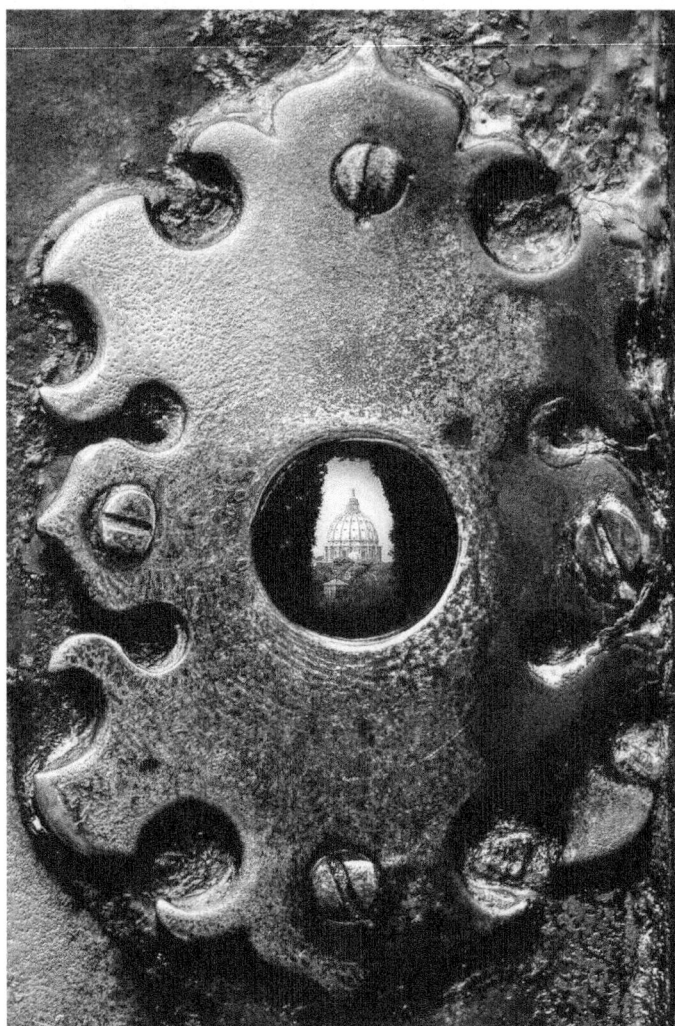

•   What It Is: Found on the massive door of the Priory of the Knights of Malta on Aventine Hill, this small, round keyhole provides a perfectly framed view of St. Peter's Basilica, nestled within a lush, symmetrical hedgerow.

•   Significance: The Priory dates back to the 10th century and is part of the Sovereign

Military Order of Malta. The alignment of the keyhole view is thought to be intentional, offering a symbolic journey through greenery to the spiritual center of Rome.

- Experience:
- Peer through the keyhole for an unforgettable and unexpected sight of St. Peter's Basilica.
- This attraction is free, though lines may form as visitors take turns to enjoy the view.

Orange Garden (Giardino degli Aranci)

•   Overview: Just a short walk from the keyhole lies the Orange Garden, or Parco Savello, a peaceful park that offers sweeping views of Rome's skyline.

•   Features:
•   The garden is filled with fragrant orange trees and benches where visitors can relax.

• A terrace at the garden's edge provides a panoramic view of the Tiber River and some of the city's most famous domes and rooftops.

• History: Originally the site of a medieval Savelli fortress, the space was converted into a public park in the 20th century.

• Tips: Sunset is the best time to visit, as the city's golden hues make the view even more stunning.

Testaccio Neighborhood and Its Culinary Scene

Overview of Testaccio

• What It Is: Testaccio, a district south of Rome's center, is a vibrant working-class neighborhood known as the birthplace of cucina romana (Roman cuisine). It offers a mix of history, authentic dining, and a lively atmosphere.

• Why It's Special: Unlike more tourist-heavy areas, Testaccio retains a local charm with its cobblestone streets, colorful murals, and bustling markets.

Historical Highlights

1. Monte dei Cocci:
• This man-made hill, created from discarded clay jars (amphorae) used in ancient Roman trade, is a striking testament to Testaccio's history as an industrial hub.

2. Pyramid of Cestius:
• An Egyptian-inspired tomb built in 12 BCE for Gaius Cestius, this pyramid stands as one of Rome's most unusual landmarks.

Culinary Scene

Testaccio is considered a foodie paradise, offering both traditional Roman dishes and innovative street food:

• Testaccio Market:

• A modern food market filled with vendors selling fresh produce, meats, and cheeses.

• Popular stalls include Mordi e Vai, known for sandwiches stuffed with Roman specialties, and Trapizzino, offering pizza dough pockets filled with slow-cooked meats.

• Traditional Trattorias:

• Flavio al Velavevodetto: Renowned for its cacio e pepe and amatriciana.

• Checchino dal 1887: A historic spot offering classic offal dishes like oxtail stew.

How to Explore

• Take a guided food tour to learn about the neighborhood's culinary traditions.

• Visit the market at lunchtime to enjoy the freshest offerings and soak up the local energy.

Underground Rome: Catacombs and Crypts

The Catacombs

Rome's catacombs are ancient underground cemeteries that reveal the burial practices and religious life of early Christians:

1.   Catacombs of San Sebastiano:

•   Located along the Appian Way, these catacombs include frescoes, inscriptions, and the tomb of St. Sebastian, a Christian martyr.

2.   Catacombs of San Callisto (St. Callixtus):

•	Known for the Crypt of the Popes, this site is the resting place of early popes and martyrs.

3.	Catacombs of Priscilla:
•	Often called the "Queen of the Catacombs," it features beautiful frescoes, including one of the earliest known depictions of the Virgin Mary.

Crypts and Ossuaries

1.	Capuchin Crypt:

• Beneath the church of Santa Maria della Concezione, this crypt is decorated with the bones of over 4,000 Capuchin friars, arranged in elaborate designs.

2.   San Clemente Basilica:
• This multi-layered site allows visitors to explore a 12th-century church, a 4th-century basilica, and a 1st-century Roman house, complete with frescoes and Mithraic altars.

Visiting Tips

• Wear sturdy shoes, as the pathways are uneven.
• Guided tours are highly recommended to fully understand the historical and spiritual significance of these sites.

Street Art and Contemporary Culture

Rome's Street Art Scene

While Rome is celebrated for its ancient art, its contemporary street art scene is equally compelling. Certain neighborhoods have become open-air galleries, showcasing colorful murals and graffiti by both local and international artists.

1.   Ostiense District:
- A former industrial area now covered in large-scale murals. Look for works by Blu, whose politically charged art is internationally recognized.

2.   Tor Marancia:
- Known as the "Big City Life" project, this residential area features stunning murals on apartment buildings, blending art with everyday life.

3.   Pigneto:
- A hip, bohemian neighborhood filled with smaller street art pieces, trendy cafes, and live music venues.

Contemporary Art Galleries

1.   MAXXI (National Museum of 21st-Century Arts):
- Designed by Zaha Hadid, this museum focuses on contemporary art and architecture.

2.   MACRO (Museum of Contemporary Art Rome):

- Located in a former brewery, MACRO showcases bold modern art installations.

How to Explore

- Join a street art walking tour to uncover the stories behind the murals.
- Combine your visit with stops at local cafes or craft beer bars in these neighborhoods.

Conclusion

Rome's hidden gems and off-the-beaten-path experiences offer a fresh perspective on the Eternal City. From the serene Aventine Keyhole and the culinary wonders of Testaccio to the haunting catacombs and vibrant street art districts, these spots provide unique ways to connect with Rome's history and modern spirit. Exploring these lesser-known treasures ensures your time in Rome is as diverse and unforgettable as the city itself.

DAY TRIP FROM ROME

Rome's central location makes it an excellent starting point for exploring nearby destinations. Beyond the city's historic landmarks, there's a world of ancient ruins, serene countryside, and beautiful beaches waiting to be discovered. These day trips allow you to experience more of Italy's culture, history, and natural beauty, complementing your time in Rome. Below is a detailed guide to four unforgettable excursions.

Tivoli: Villa d'Este and Villa Adriana

Why Visit Tivoli?

Tivoli, just 30 kilometers (19 miles) east of Rome, is a picturesque town steeped in history. It's known for its magnificent villas and lush gardens, offering a peaceful escape from the bustling city. The town has long been a retreat for Roman aristocrats and Renaissance nobility.

Villa d'Este: Renaissance Luxury

• History: Built in the 16th century by Cardinal Ippolito II d'Este, Villa d'Este is a UNESCO World Heritage Site. Its design reflects the wealth and artistic vision of the Renaissance era.

- Highlights:
- The Fountains: The villa's gardens are adorned with over 50 fountains, including the iconic Fountain of Neptune, which cascades into a shimmering pool, and the charming Hundred Fountains, a path lined with continuous streams of water.

- Terraced Gardens: Winding paths lead through manicured lawns and flowerbeds, offering stunning views of the countryside.

- Interior Frescoes: Inside, the villa features intricately painted ceilings and walls depicting mythological themes.

- Tip: Visit in the late afternoon when the light highlights the beauty of the fountains.

Villa Adriana: A Roman Emperor's Retreat

- History: Emperor Hadrian built this sprawling villa in the 2nd century AD as a luxurious getaway. Its design reflects his admiration for Greek and Egyptian architecture.

- Highlights:

- Canopus: A long pool surrounded by statues and arches, inspired by an Egyptian canal.
- Teatro Marittimo: A circular island villa believed to have been Hadrian's private retreat.

- Baths and Water Features: The villa's engineering prowess is evident in its intricate bath complexes and water systems.

- Tip: Allow at least 3 hours to explore this vast archaeological site.

How to Get to Tivoli

- By Train: A 45-minute train ride from Termini Station.
- By Car: A 40-minute drive via the A24 highway.
- Guided Tours: Many tours combine Villa d'Este and Villa Adriana, providing historical context.

Castelli Romani: Scenic Hills and Wine Culture

What Is Castelli Romani?

The Castelli Romani is a group of 13 hilltop towns in the Alban Hills, southeast of Rome. These towns are known for their lush vineyards, historic villas, and tranquil lakes, making them a popular retreat for Romans.

Frascati: The Wine Capital

- Wine Culture:
- Frascati is famous for its light, crisp white wines, often paired with local delicacies.

- Wineries: Visit estates like Casale Marchese or Cantina Santa Benedetta for tastings and vineyard tours.

- Historical Highlights:
- Villa Aldobrandini: A grand 16th-century villa with elaborate gardens.
- Cattedrale di San Pietro Apostolo: A beautiful church blending Baroque and Neoclassical styles.

Other Must-Visit Towns

1. Nemi:
- Known for its wild strawberries and stunning views of Lake Nemi.
- Visit the Museum of Roman Ships, showcasing artifacts from Emperor Caligula's vessels.

2. Ariccia:
- Famous for porchetta, a traditional roast pork dish.
- Explore Palazzo Chigi, a Baroque palace with preserved interiors.

How to Experience Castelli Romani

- By Train: A 30-minute ride from Termini Station to Frascati.
- By Car: A scenic drive along the Via Appia Antica.
- Tip: Weekends are ideal for visiting, with markets and festivals adding to the charm.

Ostia Antica: The Ancient Roman Harbor

Why Visit Ostia Antica?

Located about 30 kilometers (19 miles) southwest of Rome, Ostia Antica was the bustling port city of ancient Rome. Today, it is one of the best-preserved archaeological sites, offering a fascinating glimpse into Roman urban life.

What to See in Ostia Antica

1.   The Forum: The central square surrounded by temples and administrative buildings.

2.   The Amphitheater: A well-preserved venue for performances, seating over 4,000 people.

3.   Baths of Neptune: Featuring intricate mosaics of Neptune and sea creatures.

4.   Insulae (Apartments): Multi-story buildings showcasing the living quarters of ordinary Romans.

5.   Thermopolium: A Roman snack bar with preserved counters and storage jars.

Tips for Visiting

•   Explore at your own pace or join a guided tour to understand the significance of the ruins.

•   Bring sunscreen and water, as the site is largely outdoors.

Getting to Ostia Antica

- By Train: Take the Roma-Lido line from Porta San Paolo to Ostia Antica (30 minutes).

- By Car: A 40-minute drive via Via del Mare.

Beaches Near Rome: Sperlonga and Santa Marinella

Sperlonga: A Seaside Gem

- Overview: Located 120 kilometers (75 miles) south of Rome, Sperlonga is a picturesque coastal town known for its whitewashed houses, sandy beaches, and clear waters.

- Highlights:

• Beaches: Relax at Spiaggia di Levante or Spiaggia di Ponente, both offering calm, pristine waters.

• Villa of Tiberius: Explore the ruins of Emperor Tiberius's villa, featuring a grotto with ancient sculptures.

• Old Town: Wander narrow streets lined with boutiques and cafes.

Santa Marinella: Rome's Favorite Beach Escape

•   Overview: Just 60 kilometers (37 miles) northwest of Rome, Santa Marinella offers a family-friendly atmosphere with sandy beaches and calm seas.

•   Highlights:

- Spiaggia di Santa Marinella: A popular beach with rental facilities and cafes.
- Castello Odescalchi: A medieval castle overlooking the water.

How to Get There

- Sperlonga:
- By Train: A 1.5-hour ride from Termini to Fondi-Sperlonga, followed by a short bus ride.
- By Car: A 2-hour drive along the A1 highway.

- Santa Marinella:
- By Train: A 50-minute train ride from Termini Station.
- By Car: A 1-hour drive along the A12 highway.

Tips for Day Trips

1. Plan Ahead: Check train schedules and entry times for attractions.
2. Pack Essentials: Comfortable shoes, sunscreen, water, and a light jacket are must-haves.
3. Consider Tours: Guided tours often provide transportation and detailed insights.

ACCOMMODATION

Rome offers a wide variety of accommodations to suit every traveler's needs, from budget-friendly hostels to luxurious historic palaces. Choosing the right neighborhood and accommodation type can enhance your experience and ensure a memorable stay. Here's an in-depth guide to help you decide where to stay in Rome.

Types of Accommodation

Hotels

Rome's hotels range from affordable 2-star options to opulent 5-star luxury establishments. Many are housed in historic buildings, combining old-world charm with modern amenities.

Boutique Hotels

Boutique hotels in Rome often feature unique, stylish interiors and personalized service. These are ideal for travelers seeking a more intimate experience.

Guesthouses and Bed & Breakfasts

Guesthouses and B&Bs are popular for their homey atmosphere and affordability. Many are run by locals, providing insight into Roman culture.

Apartments and Vacation Rentals

Vacation rentals are great for families or longer stays. Platforms like Airbnb and Vrbo offer a range of options, from studio apartments to spacious homes.

Hostels

Budget travelers and backpackers can choose from a variety of hostels offering dormitory beds and private rooms. Some even include free breakfast or social events.

Best Neighborhoods to Stay in Rome

Choosing the right neighborhood in Rome is essential for an enjoyable stay, whether you're drawn to history, shopping, nightlife, or peaceful retreats. Each area offers its own unique charm, proximity to major attractions, and a variety of accommodations to suit different budgets. Here's a detailed guide to the best neighborhoods to stay in Rome:

1. Centro Storico (Historic Center)

Why Stay Here?

The Centro Storico is the heart of Rome, filled with iconic landmarks, narrow cobblestone streets, charming piazzas, and lively cafes. Staying here places you within walking distance of major attractions like the Pantheon, Piazza Navona, and the Trevi Fountain.

Key Features

- Attractions: The Pantheon, Piazza Navona, Campo de' Fiori, and the Trevi Fountain.
- Atmosphere: Romantic, bustling, and steeped in history.
- Dining: A mix of traditional trattorias and upscale dining options.
- Best For: First-time visitors and those who want to experience Rome's historic charm up close.

Downsides

- Can be crowded and noisy, especially during peak tourist seasons.
- Accommodations are often more expensive due to the prime location.

2. Trastevere

Why Stay Here?

Trastevere, located just across the Tiber River, is one of Rome's most picturesque and bohemian neighborhoods. It offers a lively yet laid-back vibe with charming streets, excellent restaurants, and a vibrant nightlife.

Key Features

- Attractions: Santa Maria in Trastevere, Janiculum Hill, and Villa Farnesina.
- Atmosphere: Artistic, authentic, and cozy, with ivy-covered buildings and hidden courtyards.
- Dining: Home to some of the best Roman trattorias and pizzerias, including local favorites like Trattoria Da Enzo al 29.
- Best For: Couples, foodies, and those looking for a mix of local culture and nightlife.

Downsides

- Slightly removed from major attractions like the Colosseum or Vatican City.
- Cobblestone streets can be challenging for those with heavy luggage or mobility issues.

3. Vatican City and Prati

Why Stay Here?

Perfect for visitors who want to explore Vatican City, including St. Peter's Basilica, the Vatican Museums, and the Sistine Chapel. The nearby Prati district is elegant and less touristy, offering wide streets, boutique shops, and great restaurants.

Key Features

- Attractions: Vatican City, Castel Sant'Angelo, and Piazza San Pietro.
- Atmosphere: Quiet, clean, and upscale, with a residential feel.
- Dining: A mix of authentic Roman eateries and modern cafes.
- Best For: Pilgrims, art lovers, and travelers seeking a tranquil yet central location.

Downsides

- Less nightlife compared to areas like Trastevere or Campo de' Fiori.
- Somewhat distant from attractions in the historic center.

4. Monti

Why Stay Here?

Monti is a trendy and centrally located neighborhood with a village-like atmosphere. Its winding streets are lined with artisan shops, hip cafes, and vintage boutiques. It's within walking distance of the Colosseum and Roman Forum.

Key Features

- Attractions: Colosseum, Roman Forum, and Basilica di Santa Maria Maggiore.
- Atmosphere: Chic, bohemian, and youthful, with a mix of old-world charm and modern vibes.
- Dining: A hotspot for gourmet dining, wine bars, and casual eateries.
- Best For: Young travelers, solo adventurers, and anyone looking for a stylish, central location.

Downsides

- Streets can be steep and uneven, which may be challenging for some.
- Accommodations can be boutique-style, with fewer large hotels.

5. Testaccio

Why Stay Here?

Testaccio is a food lover's paradise and one of the most authentic Roman neighborhoods. Known for its traditional markets and culinary heritage, it's less touristy than the historic center but still offers easy access to key attractions.

Key Features

- Attractions: Pyramid of Cestius, Protestant Cemetery, and Testaccio Market.
- Atmosphere: Local and lively, with a strong focus on food and tradition.
- Dining: Famous for classic Roman dishes like cacio e pepe and carbonara.
- Best For: Food enthusiasts and those seeking a more local experience.

Downsides

- Limited major tourist attractions compared to other neighborhoods.
- Nightlife is lively but more localized, not ideal for those seeking upscale entertainment.

6. Campo de' Fiori

Why Stay Here?

This central neighborhood is known for its lively square, bustling daily market, and vibrant nightlife. It's within walking distance of the historic center, making it convenient for sightseeing.

Key Features

- Attractions: Campo de' Fiori Market, Piazza Farnese, and nearby Piazza Navona.
- Atmosphere: Bustling during the day with a more relaxed vibe in the evening.
- Dining: A mix of casual eateries and trendy restaurants.
- Best For: Night owls, market lovers, and travelers who enjoy vibrant city life.

Downsides

- Can be noisy, especially in the evenings due to nightlife.
- Accommodations may be more limited compared to nearby Centro Storico.

7. Esquilino

Why Stay Here?

Esquilino, one of Rome's seven hills, is a diverse and multicultural area close to Termini Station, making it ideal for travelers relying on public transport. The neighborhood is rich in history and features beautiful churches and ancient ruins.

Key Features

- Attractions: Basilica di Santa Maria Maggiore, Piazza Vittorio Emanuele II, and the National Roman Museum.
- Atmosphere: Diverse and bustling, with a mix of local and international influences.
- Dining: Affordable eateries and multicultural cuisine options.
- Best For: Budget-conscious travelers and those needing quick access to transportation.

Downsides

- Less charming than other neighborhoods; some areas may feel less safe at night.
- Not as scenic or romantic as Trastevere or Centro Storico.

8. Piazza di Spagna (Spanish Steps)

Why Stay Here?

This luxurious area around the Spanish Steps and Via Condotti is ideal for shoppers and those seeking elegance. It offers high-end hotels, boutique shopping, and easy access to major attractions.

Key Features

- Attractions: Spanish Steps, Villa Borghese Gardens, and Trevi Fountain.
- Atmosphere: Upscale, fashionable, and sophisticated.
- Dining: Gourmet restaurants, chic cafes, and stylish bars.
- Best For: Luxury travelers and those seeking a central, high-end experience.

Downsides

- Accommodations are pricey, reflecting the neighborhood's exclusivity.
- Can be crowded with tourists during the day.

9. Aventine Hill

Why Stay Here?

Aventine Hill offers a peaceful and serene escape from the bustling city while still being close to key attractions like the Colosseum and Circus Maximus. Known for its lush gardens and quiet streets, it's perfect for a romantic getaway.

Key Features

- Attractions: Orange Garden (Giardino degli Aranci), Keyhole of Rome, and Santa Sabina Basilica.
- Atmosphere: Tranquil, residential, and scenic.
- Dining: Quaint local restaurants and cafes.
- Best For: Couples, families, and those seeking a quiet retreat.

Downsides

- Limited nightlife and dining options compared to livelier neighborhoods.
- Less public transport access, so walking or taxis may be necessary.

Tips for Choosing a Neighborhood in Rome

- First-Time Visitors: Centro Storico, Monti, or Trastevere for proximity to major attractions and vibrant atmospheres.
- Budget Travelers: Esquilino or Testaccio for affordable accommodations and dining.
- Luxury Seekers: Piazza di Spagna or Aventine Hill for upscale experiences.
- Food Enthusiasts: Trastevere or Testaccio for exceptional dining options.
- Quiet Retreat: Aventine Hill or Prati for a peaceful stay.

Budget Options

1. Esquilino

Why It's Budget-Friendly:
Esquilino is one of the most affordable neighborhoods in central Rome, thanks to its

proximity to Termini Station, the city's main transportation hub. The area offers plenty of budget accommodations, including hostels, mid-range hotels, and guesthouses, as well as affordable dining options.

Key Features:
- Attractions Nearby: Basilica di Santa Maria Maggiore, Piazza Vittorio Emanuele II, and the National Roman Museum.
- Dining: Esquilino is a multicultural area, offering a mix of traditional Roman trattorias and international cuisine at wallet-friendly prices.
- Convenience: Excellent access to Rome's public transportation network, including metro lines, buses, and trains.

Who Should Stay Here:
Budget-conscious travelers and backpackers who prioritize affordability and accessibility to public transport.

Recommended Budget Hotels/Hostels in Esquilino:
- Generator Rome: A stylish, modern hostel with private and shared rooms, close to Termini Station.
- Hotel Sweet Home: A cozy, budget-friendly option with a central location.

- The Beehive: An eco-friendly hostel offering dorms and private rooms with a laid-back vibe.

2. Testaccio

Why It's Budget-Friendly:

Testaccio is a lesser-known yet vibrant neighborhood south of the historic center. It offers a more local and authentic Roman experience at a fraction of the cost of areas like Trastevere or Centro Storico. Accommodations are reasonably priced, and the dining scene focuses on affordable traditional Roman cuisine.

Key Features:

- Attractions Nearby: Pyramid of Cestius, Protestant Cemetery, and Testaccio Market.
- Dining: Known as a food lover's haven, Testaccio has many family-run trattorias and eateries offering excellent value for money. Dishes like cacio e pepe and carciofi alla romana are must-tries.
- Authenticity: A residential vibe with fewer tourists and a strong connection to Roman culinary traditions.

Who Should Stay Here:

Food enthusiasts, travelers seeking a local experience, and those looking for an affordable yet authentic Roman neighborhood.

Recommended Budget Hotels/Apartments in Testaccio:

- Hotel Re Testa: A modern hotel with affordable rates and spacious rooms.

- RomeHello B&B: A cozy and affordable bed-and-breakfast with a welcoming atmosphere.

- Airbnb Options: Many budget apartments are available in Testaccio, often with kitchens to save on dining costs.

3. San Lorenzo

Why It's Budget-Friendly:

San Lorenzo is a youthful, artsy neighborhood near the Sapienza University of Rome, making it popular among students and budget travelers. Accommodations here are among the cheapest in central Rome, and the area is filled with inexpensive eateries and vibrant nightlife.

Key Features:

- Attractions Nearby: Porta Maggiore, Basilica di San Lorenzo fuori le Mura, and ancient Roman aqueduct ruins.
- Dining: Affordable pizzerias, cafes, and gelaterias dominate the food scene here, catering to students and locals.
- Nightlife: The neighborhood comes alive at night with bars, live music venues, and casual spots perfect for socializing.

Who Should Stay Here:
Young travelers, solo adventurers, and anyone looking for budget accommodations in a lively, creative neighborhood.

Recommended Budget Hotels/Hostels in San Lorenzo:
- Roma Scout Center: A unique and budget-friendly hostel in a peaceful area near the neighborhood.

- YellowSquare Rome: A trendy hostel with dorms and private rooms, a bar, and social events.

- Albergo Athena: A simple yet affordable hotel option, ideal for budget-conscious travelers.

Tips for Budget Travelers in Rome:

1.   Choose Accommodations with Kitchens: Stay in hostels or Airbnb apartments to cook your meals and save on dining expenses.

2.   Use Public Transport: Rome's metro and bus systems are inexpensive and well-connected to most neighborhoods.

3.   Avoid Peak Tourist Seasons: Travel during the off-season (November to March) for lower accommodation prices.

4.   Stay Outside the City Center: Neighborhoods like Testaccio, Esquilino, and San Lorenzo offer better value for money while still being close to major attractions.

Mid-Range and Boutique Hotels in Rome

Rome has plenty of mid-range and boutique hotels that offer a great mix of affordability, comfort, and style. Whether you want to stay in a charming, historic area, enjoy modern facilities, or have a personalized experience, there are options to suit your needs. Here's a simple guide to help you find the best places.

1. Centro Storico (Historic Center)

Why Stay Here

The historic center is perfect for soaking up Rome's charm, with its old streets, beautiful churches, and famous landmarks. Hotels in this area often combine historic architecture with modern comforts.

Top Hotels

1.   Hotel Navona: Near Piazza Navona and the Pantheon, this hotel is in a restored historic building with rooms that mix Roman decor and modern features. Great for history lovers.
   • Perks: Free Wi-Fi, breakfast, and helpful staff.

2.   Albergo del Senato: Right across from the Pantheon, this hotel has elegant interiors and stunning views. Ideal for couples.
   • Perks: Rooftop terrace, soundproof rooms, free breakfast.

3.   Hotel Smeraldo: Close to Campo de' Fiori, this cozy hotel has stylish, modern rooms with a boutique vibe. Perfect for active travelers.

- Perks: Rooftop terrace, 24/7 front desk, family-friendly rooms.

2. Trastevere

Why Stay Here

This charming neighborhood offers an authentic Roman vibe with its lively streets, historic character, and great restaurants. Boutique hotels here are often in historic buildings with lots of personality.

Top Hotels

1. VOI Donna Camilla Savelli Hotel: A former 17th-century convent designed by Borromini, this hotel blends historical charm with luxury. Ideal for couples and history fans.
   - Perks: Beautiful gardens, on-site restaurant, elegant rooms.

2. Hotel San Francesco: A boutique hotel near the Tiber River with modern, stylish rooms. Perfect for a quiet escape in a lively area.
   - Perks: Rooftop terrace, free breakfast, cozy bar.

3. Relais Le Clarisse: A hidden gem with quaint courtyards and well-designed rooms, offering a peaceful, intimate setting.
- Perks: Free Wi-Fi, breakfast, garden.

3. Monti

Why Stay Here

Monti is trendy and artistic, known for its boutique shops and cafes. It's also close to the Colosseum and Roman Forum, making it great for sightseeing.

Top Hotels

1. The Fifteen Keys Hotel: A stylish boutique hotel with modern decor in the heart of Monti. Perfect for design lovers.
- Perks: Personalized service, breakfast, peaceful garden.

2. Palazzo Manfredi: A luxury boutique hotel with incredible views of the Colosseum. Great for couples wanting a special experience.
- Perks: Michelin-starred restaurant, rooftop terrace, elegant rooms.

3. Hotel Grifo: A welcoming mid-range hotel on a quiet street, ideal for families or solo travelers.
- Perks: Free breakfast, terrace, pet-friendly options.

4. Prati

Why Stay Here

Close to Vatican City, Prati is an elegant area with wide streets and boutique shops. It's quieter than the city center but still well-connected to major attractions.

Top Hotels

1. Hotel Giulio Cesare: A family-run hotel offering a mix of classic and modern decor. Ideal for families or business trips.
- Perks: Free breakfast, garden terrace, spacious rooms.

2. Relais Vatican View: A modern boutique hotel just steps from St. Peter's Basilica. Great for couples or pilgrims.
- Perks: Rooftop terrace with Vatican views, free Wi-Fi, kitchenette options.

3. NH Collection Roma Giustiniano: A contemporary hotel with a central location, perfect for business travelers or families.
- Perks: Fitness center, free breakfast, pet-friendly.

5. Aventine Hill

Why Stay Here

This peaceful neighborhood is perfect for travelers seeking a quiet, scenic retreat with lovely views.

Top Hotels

1. Hotel Aventino: A charming boutique hotel surrounded by lush gardens, ideal for couples or nature lovers.
- Perks: Free parking, breakfast, garden access.

2. Villa San Pio: A romantic hotel with garden-facing rooms and a serene atmosphere. Perfect for honeymooners or families.
- Perks: Free breakfast, private balconies, family rooms.

3.   Domus Aventina: Located near the Orange Garden, this cozy hotel offers a mix of history and comfort.
•   Perks: Free Wi-Fi, breakfast, quiet ambiance.

6. Campo de' Fiori

Why Stay Here

This lively area is known for its market, nightlife, and proximity to major attractions like Piazza Navona and the Pantheon.

Top Hotels

1.   Hotel Campo de' Fiori: A boutique hotel with uniquely styled rooms and a rooftop terrace offering stunning views. Great for travelers who enjoy a vibrant atmosphere.
•   Perks: Free Wi-Fi, breakfast, personal concierge service.

2.   Residenza Zanardelli: A boutique guesthouse offering affordable luxury near Piazza Navona. Perfect for couples and solo travelers.
•   Perks: Free breakfast, modern amenities, central location.

Why Choose a Boutique Hotel?

•	Personal Touch: Boutique hotels focus on fewer guests, so the service feels more personal.

•	Unique Design: Each hotel is distinct, often featuring decor inspired by Roman culture and history.

•	Historic Charm: Many are housed in historic buildings, giving you a deeper connection to the city's past.

Tips for Picking a Hotel

1.	Book Early: Boutique hotels have limited rooms, so reserve in advance, especially during busy seasons.

2.	Check Amenities: Look for hotels with free breakfast, Wi-Fi, and convenient transport options.

3.	Choose a Location: Stay near the attractions you plan to visit but consider the vibe of the neighborhood.

4.	Read Reviews: Check guest reviews on Booking.com or TripAdvisor to get real insights

Luxury Hotels and Historic Residences in Rome

If you're looking for top-notch comfort and elegance, Rome has plenty of options. The city's luxury hotels and historic residences combine world-class service with stunning architecture and prime locations, giving you a memorable stay.

1. Hotel Eden (Centro Storico)

- Overview: Hotel Eden is a 5-star hotel in the heart of Rome near the Spanish Steps. It offers stunning views of the city and a mix of modern luxury and classic charm.

- Key Features:
- A Michelin-starred restaurant, La Terrazza, with amazing city views.
- Luxurious, stylish rooms and suites with high-end amenities.
- A relaxing spa with personalized treatments.

- Who Should Stay: Couples, families, and anyone wanting a luxury experience with great views.

- Why Stay Here: Its excellent location, high-end services, and breathtaking views make it a standout choice.

2. Palazzo Manfredi (Colosseum)

- Overview: This boutique hotel is right next to the Colosseum, offering a unique blend of luxury and history. You'll wake up to incredible views of ancient Rome.

- Key Features:
- Suites with large windows overlooking the Colosseum.
- A Michelin-starred rooftop restaurant, Aroma, serving gourmet cuisine.
- Personalized concierge services, including private tours.

- Who Should Stay: Couples and history enthusiasts who want to combine luxury with cultural experiences.

- Why Stay Here: The unbeatable views and its location make it a perfect choice for a memorable stay in Rome.

3. St. Regis Rome (Esquilino)

- Overview: Located in the Esquilino district, the St. Regis Rome is a historic hotel known for its grand interiors and exceptional service. Opened in 1894, it's a favorite for guests who appreciate tradition and luxury.

- Key Features:
- Lavish rooms with a mix of classic and modern styles.
- Personalized St. Regis Butler Service for a unique experience.
- A chic lounge and bar, plus a luxurious spa.

- Who Should Stay: Travelers who want a mix of history, comfort, and personalized service.

- Why Stay Here: Its elegant design and attention to detail make it one of the best luxury hotels in Rome.

4. Residenza Ruspoli Bonaparte (Centro Storico)

- Overview: This historic palace, once home to Napoleon Bonaparte's family, offers a royal living experience in central Rome. It's perfect for travelers who love history and charm.

- Key Features:
- Antique furniture, frescoed ceilings, and historic decor.
- A small, boutique atmosphere with personalized attention.
- Close to landmarks like Piazza Navona and the Pantheon.

- Who Should Stay: History lovers or anyone looking for a unique, private experience.

- Why Stay Here: Staying here feels like stepping back in time, while still enjoying modern luxuries.

Why Stay in a Luxury Hotel or Historic Residence?

- Top Service: These places offer personalized services like private tours, fine dining, and 24/7 assistance.

- Beautiful Buildings: Many are located in historic palaces or villas with stunning decor.

- Great Locations: They're often near Rome's most famous landmarks.

- Special Experiences: From rooftop dining to relaxing spa treatments, these hotels go beyond just a place to sleep.

Tips for Booking

1. Plan Ahead: Luxury accommodations are popular, especially during peak travel seasons, so book early.

2. Know Your Priorities: Decide if you want great views, proximity to landmarks, or historic charm.

3. Look for Packages: Some hotels include extras like tours or spa treatments.

4. Check Reviews: Look up guest reviews to find the perfect match for your needs.

Tips for Picking the Right Place to Stay in Rome

Choosing the right accommodation can make your trip to Rome more enjoyable. Whether you're visiting for the first time, traveling with family, or on a budget, these tips will help you find the perfect place.

1. Know What You Need

Different neighborhoods in Rome suit different types of travelers:

- First-Time Visitors: Stay in Centro Storico or near Piazza Navona for easy access to famous spots like the Pantheon and Trevi Fountain.
- Families: Pick quieter areas like Trastevere or Prati, which have a peaceful vibe and are close to parks or the Vatican.
- Budget Travelers: Look in neighborhoods like Termini or Esquilino for affordable options and good public transport connections.
- Luxury Travelers: Choose upscale areas such as the Spanish Steps or Aventine Hill, which offer plenty of high-end hotels and historic residences.

2. Book Early

Rome is a popular tourist destination all year, so accommodations fill up quickly:

- Plan Ahead: Book 3-6 months in advance, especially if you're traveling during busy seasons like spring or autumn.

- Special Events: For big occasions like Easter, Christmas, or Vatican events, reserve even earlier to secure your stay.

3. Check the Amenities

Make sure your accommodation has the facilities you need for a comfortable stay:
- Wi-Fi: Essential for trip planning and navigation.
- Air Conditioning: A must during the hot summer months (June to September).
- Breakfast: Many hotels include breakfast, which can save you time and money.
- Elevators: Some older buildings might not have them, so confirm if this is important for you.
- 24-Hour Reception: Handy if you're arriving late or leaving early.

4. Read Reviews

Before booking, check what past guests have said about the property:
- Trusted Platforms: Use websites like TripAdvisor, Booking.com, or Google Reviews.
- Key Details: Focus on reviews mentioning cleanliness, noise levels, and how helpful the staff is.

- Recent Feedback: Make sure the reviews are up-to-date to ensure the property still meets high standards.

5. Stay Near Public Transport

Rome's metro, bus, and tram systems make getting around easy, so staying near public transport is a big plus:
- Convenient Metro Stops: Stations like Termini, Spagna (Spanish Steps), or Ottaviano (Vatican) are ideal.
- Bus and Tram Access: If you're staying in areas like Trastevere or Testaccio, ensure there's a nearby bus or tram stop.

6. Balance Location and Price

Think about how much you're willing to spend and where you want to be:
- Central Areas: Staying in the city center is convenient for walking to attractions but can be more expensive.
- Outer Neighborhoods: Areas like San Giovanni or Testaccio are quieter, more affordable, and still close to public transport.

7. Look for Deals

Hotels often run special offers that can save you money or add value to your stay:
- Promotions: Check for discounts during low seasons or offers for longer stays.
- Packages: Some deals include extras like breakfast, airport transfers, or guided tours.
- Direct Bookings: Sometimes, booking directly with the hotel gets you better rates or perks.

8. Match Your Travel Style

Choose a place that fits how you like to travel:
- Independent Travelers: Apartments or Airbnbs give you more privacy and the option to cook your own meals.
- Social Travelers: Hostels or guesthouses are great for meeting new people.
- Luxury Travelers: Boutique hotels or historic residences offer a high-end, unique experience.

9. Be Prepared for City Taxes

Rome has a city tax that ranges from €3 to €7 per person per night, depending on the type of accommodation. This tax is not included in the booking price and must be paid directly at check-in or check-out.

Final Tip

By considering your needs, planning ahead, and checking reviews, you can find the perfect accommodation to suit your style and budget, making your trip to Rome even more enjoyable.

SIMPLE INSIDER TIPS

Rome is a city full of wonders, and with some insider knowledge, you can make your visit smoother, more enjoyable, and less crowded. Here's a practical guide to help you explore Rome, avoid common hassles, and experience the city like a local.

1. Skip the Lines at Major Attractions

The top attractions in Rome can get crowded, but here's how to avoid wasting time in long lines:
- Book Tickets Ahead:
- Visit the official websites for places like the Colosseum, Roman Forum, and Vatican Museums to buy skip-the-line or timed-entry tickets.

- Join a Guided Tour:
- Many tours offer priority entry and early or after-hours access. Some Colosseum tours even include the underground tunnels or arena floor for a unique experience.

- Use Multi-Attraction Passes:
- Cards like the Roma Pass or Omnia Vatican Card include fast-track entry to multiple

sites and public transport. The Archaeological Card covers key ancient ruins like the Colosseum and Palatine Hill.

• Visit During Off-Peak Times:
• Arrive early when attractions open or visit in the late afternoon. Weekdays are less busy than weekends.

• Pro Tip for St. Peter's Basilica:
• Skip the long security line by booking a Vatican Museums tour that ends directly inside the basilica.

2. Best Times to Visit Popular Spots

Timing can make a huge difference in your experience. Plan your visits wisely:
• Choose the Right Season:
• Spring (April-May) and autumn (September-October) are perfect for good weather and fewer crowds.
• Winter (November-February) is quieter and cheaper, except for the holiday season. Avoid the hot and crowded summer months (July-August).

• Plan Your Day:

- Visit popular spots like the Vatican Museums or Colosseum as soon as they open (usually 8:30 AM).
- Explore open-air sites like the Trevi Fountain or Piazza Navona in the evening when they're beautifully lit and less crowded.

- Nighttime Visits:
- Many landmarks, like the Colosseum, offer special night tours. This is a quieter, cooler, and more magical way to experience Rome.

3. Explore Local Neighborhoods Beyond the Crowds

Rome isn't just about famous landmarks. Step away from the tourist spots to discover its authentic side:
- Testaccio:
- A food lover's paradise with authentic trattorias, the lively Testaccio Market, and traditional Roman dishes like cacio e pepe.

- Trastevere:
- A charming area with cobblestone streets, family-run restaurants, and hidden gems like the Santa Maria in Trastevere church.

- San Lorenzo:

- A trendy, student-friendly district filled with street art, affordable cafes, and a lively atmosphere.

- Pigneto:
- Known for its hip, creative vibe, this district has plenty of trendy bars, experimental restaurants, and a buzzing nightlife.

- Monteverde:
- A peaceful residential area with access to Villa Doria Pamphili, the largest park in Rome, perfect for picnics and scenic walks.

4. Use Apps to Navigate Like a Local

Rome's streets and public transport can be confusing, but these apps make it easier:
- Google Maps:
- Great for walking directions and finding public transport options.

- Moovit or ATAC Roma:
- Real-time updates for buses, trams, and metro services.

- TheFork:
- Reserve tables at restaurants and find discounts.

- Visit a City:
- Pre-made itineraries and attraction tips for easy planning.

- Audio Guide Apps:
- Apps like Rick Steves Audio Europe or VoiceMap provide excellent self-guided tours for landmarks.

- Taxi Apps:
- Use FreeNow or ItTaxi to book taxis safely and avoid overcharging.

5. Dine and Relax Like a Local

Rome's food and parks are some of its best-kept secrets. Here's where to go:
- Local Restaurants:
- Avoid tourist traps near landmarks. Instead, head to places like Da Enzo al 29 in Trastevere for classic Roman dishes or Roscioli near Campo de' Fiori for gourmet cuisine.

- Authentic Gelato:
- Look for artisanal spots like Gelateria del Teatro or La Romana. Skip brightly colored gelato shops, which are often touristy.

- Coffee Spots:
- Try Sant'Eustachio Il Caffè or Tazza d'Oro near the Pantheon for a proper Roman espresso.

- Parks and Green Spaces:
- Relax at Villa Borghese Gardens, enjoy the views from the Orange Garden on Aventine Hill, or visit Janiculum Hill for panoramic cityscapes.

6. Making the Most of a Short Stay

If your time in Rome is limited, follow these steps to see the best highlights:
- Focus on the Essentials:
- Key spots include the Colosseum, Roman Forum, Vatican Museums, and St. Peter's Basilica.

- Use Skip-the-Line Tickets:
- Save precious time by booking in advance.

- Group Attractions by Area:
- Visit the Colosseum, Roman Forum, and Palatine Hill in the morning. Spend your afternoon exploring Piazza Navona, the Pantheon, and the Trevi Fountain.

- Stay Central:
- Book accommodations in Centro Storico or Trastevere to minimize travel time.

- Evening Strolls:
- Walk through beautifully lit landmarks like the Trevi Fountain and Piazza Venezia at night for a magical atmosphere.

- Add a Day Trip:
- If you have an extra day, consider a quick trip to Ostia Antica or Villa Adriana in Tivoli for ancient ruins and peaceful surroundings.

ICONIC ATTRACTIONS ADDRESS/GPS

1.　Colosseum
- Address: Piazza del Colosseo, 1, 00184 Rome, Italy
- Coordinates: 41.8902° N, 12.4922° E

2.　Roman Forum
- Address: Via della Salara Vecchia, 5/6, 00186 Rome, Italy
- Coordinates: 41.8925° N, 12.4853° E

3.　Pantheon
- Address: Piazza della Rotonda, 00186 Rome, Italy
- Coordinates: 41.8986° N, 12.4769° E

4.　Trevi Fountain
- Address: Piazza di Trevi, 00187 Rome, Italy
- Coordinates: 41.9009° N, 12.4833° E

5.　St. Peter's Basilica
- Address: Piazza San Pietro, 00120 Vatican City
- Coordinates: 41.9022° N, 12.4539° E

6.   Vatican Museums
*   Address: Viale   Vaticano,   00165
Rome, Italy
*   Coordinates: 41.9065° N, 12.4536° E

7.   Sistine Chapel
*   Address: Città del Vaticano, 00120
Vatican City
*   Coordinates: 41.9029° N, 12.4545° E

8.   Piazza Navona
*   Address: Piazza   Navona,   00186
Rome, Italy
*   Coordinates: 41.8989° N, 12.4731° E

9.   Spanish Steps
*   Address: Piazza di Spagna, 00187
Rome, Italy
*   Coordinates: 41.9057° N, 12.4823° E

10.   Castel Sant'Angelo
*   Address: Lungotevere Castello, 50,
00193 Rome, Italy
*   Coordinates: 41.9031° N, 12.4663° E

11.   Piazza del Popolo
*   Address: Piazza del Popolo,   00187
Rome, Italy

- Coordinates: 41.9109° N, 12.4768° E

12. Campo de' Fiori
- Address: Piazza Campo de' Fiori, 00186 Rome, Italy
  - Coordinates: 41.8956° N, 12.4722° E

13. Basilica di Santa Maria Maggiore
- Address: Piazza di Santa Maria Maggiore, 00100 Rome, Italy
  - Coordinates: 41.8978° N, 12.4984° E

14. Circus Maximus
- Address: Via del Circo Massimo, 00186 Rome, Italy
  - Coordinates: 41.8852° N, 12.4855° E

15. Palatine Hill
- Address: Via di San Gregorio, 30, 00186 Rome, Italy
  - Coordinates: 41.8894° N, 12.4882° E

16. Basilica of San Clemente
- Address: Via Labicana, 95, 00184 Rome, Italy
  - Coordinates: 41.8903° N, 12.4963° E

17. Villa Borghese Gardens

- Address: Piazzale Napoleone I, 00197 Rome, Italy
  - Coordinates: 41.9122° N, 12.4923° E

18. Basilica of St. John Lateran
- Address: Piazza di San Giovanni in Laterano, 4, 00184 Rome, Italy
  - Coordinates: 41.8858° N, 12.5063° E

19. Appian Way (Via Appia Antica)
- Address: Via Appia Antica, 00178 Rome, Italy
  - Coordinates: 41.8579° N, 12.5226° E

20. Baths of Caracalla
- Address: Viale delle Terme di Caracalla, 00153 Rome, Italy
  - Coordinates: 41.8793° N, 12.4922° E

These coordinates and addresses should help you locate Rome's iconic attractions with ease.

Printed in Great Britain
by Amazon